Shooting Stars At Sky | The Poetry of Play

SHOOTING STARS AT SKY

THE POETRY OF PLAY

Edited by Mike Bonifer

Shooting Stars At Sky | The Poetry of Play Anthology
© 2025, Edited by Mike Bonifer
ISBN: 979-8-9893829-8-9

Published by Mama's Kitchen Press
Austin, TX / Los Angeles, CA
mamaskitchenpress.com

First Trade Paperback Original Edition, 2025

Printed in the United States of America

Edited by Mike Bonifer
Layout Design by Krystle May Statler
Cover Design by Mike Bonifer and Krystle May Statler

For the tennis players at Ladera Park.
—*Mike Bonifer*

For the girls who learned double dutch
at Miracle Baptist Christian School.
—*Camari Carter Hawkins*

Contents

LEGENDARY GAMES

HEROIC PLAY

INNERPLAY

DANGEROUS GAMES

BEAUTIFUL PLAY

Foreword

As a boy growing up on a small family farm in Indiana, basketball was my obsession. Many of my earliest memories involve playing, watching and dreaming about the game. Many of the first stories I told were, as for countless beginners on countless journeys, those I told myself while shooting hoops by myself on the farm. Broadcasts of games with me making the winning basket. Accounts of incredible teams I played on, with teammates like Oscar Robertson, Wilt Chamberlain, Dave Small of our local high school team, the Ireland Spuds, Rick Mount of the Purdue Boilermakers and the Van Arsdale twins of the Indiana Hoosiers. If I remember correctly, we were undefeated, and I was the best player on those teams.

Reality had a lot of work to do to convince me I would never be in my imaginary teammates' league.

At the age of ten, I got obsessed with the sport of football. My brother, Mark, and I shared a football uniform and a helmet. I would dress up in this uniform on fall weekends and play one-boy football games in our front yard. Inspired by the Disney TV movie, *Moochie of Pop Warner Football* (game-winning play: The Skillymooch!) I assembled and captained an imaginary team, the Patoka Valley Raiders, who played other fictional youth teams from around Southern Indiana. It got to the point where I was reporting the results of our games to boys in my grade school class. Naturally, we were kicking ass weekly, and I was the star. Until one classmate, Kenny, told me his parents were going to bring him to my next game, which I'd told him we'd be playing in our league's most distant city, Evansville, in its biggest stadium, Bosse Field. Uh-oh. Kenny's older brother, Billy, didn't buy it. He cornered me one day at recess. "You're not on any football team. You're a *liar*," he taunted. Point taken. The Patoka Valley Raiders youth football franchise folded that day along with the rest of the league.

Truth had a lot of work to do before I'd learn the difference between entertaining fiction and imaginative deception.

Then one day, many years later, I began writing poetry, including, naturally enough, poetry about sports and play. It occurred to me that surely other poets have also written poetry depicting playful memories and experiences like mine. When I suggested to Hiram Sims, the extraordinary Los Angeles poet-entrepreneur, that an anthology of such poetry might be possible, he said, "Call Camari." He meant our friend, Camari Carter Hawkins, founder of Mama's Kitchen Press. Camari agreed. This book, a wondrous collection created by a gifted group of 55 poets, came from our collaboration. We made a good team, these poets, Camari and I. You could say that we played this book into existence, and that together, we have had ourselves a winning season.

Reality and Truth have at last made their way and had their say. They express themselves most profoundly in works of art like the poetry you'll discover in *Shooting Stars At Sky*.

Skillymooch!

—Mike Bonifer
26 August 2024

SHOOTING STARS AT SKY

THE POETRY OF PLAY

CHILD'S PLAY

Double Dutch Dreams

Camari Carter Hawkins

Blessed are aged knees that knew
Double Dutch Dance
Two-step
Criss-cross
Long-legged
Slew-footed
Pigeon-toed
Ghetto flamenco

Praise ears that knew
how to pick a good turner
based on the click-clack song
Beads that whacked
concrete pavement

Worship the voice
Loud and tribal
Gig-a-lo
Yo mama
K-i-s-s-i-n-g
Calling out what we thought we knew
about adulting

We loved butterflies—
never a butterfly turner.
Rhythm must be perfect
one-and-two-and
anything less takes you out
before you even started

Alliances formed
between jumper and turner
We learned how to bribe on these recess streets
Honeybun for a perfect beaded beat
made sure I twirled on my haters for 30 seconds or longer

Faces snarled if you lasted two minutes
Called me double dutchess
Everyone wanted to out-bead me then

This is where I understood how life worked
Make alliances in this world
trade skills
turn together
don't shine too much
unless you are prepared for the burn
Someone is always a few steps
behind you
Better train your ear to find
the best beaded beat for your life
once you do
never stop jumping for your dreams

Over the Line

Mike Sonksen

We used to play Over the Line, it's like baseball without the bases just hitting the ball & fielding, we'd play at Jacob Park especially around freshman year. Catching a high fly ball or hitting one over your friend's head, summer hang sessions were about running, being active. Within a year we were chasing girls trying to go to parties but at 14 we played until the street lights came on, we felt invincible on warm evenings riding bikes to Seal Beach, straight south on Norwalk Boulevard or pedaling on the riverbed past the wetlands to the other side of the 605, we'd ride with the wind

Hide and Seek

Molimau Andrew Fatu

I didn't run the fastest, but was strategic in my approach
Would hide close to home base
Had a better chance to get there with my long strides
My long arms would reach in time to tag the base

I feel that is how I lived my life
Always having a strategy to use my strengths
To mask my weaknesses, instead of working on them
Sit in the back of the class and only raise my hand if I have the answer
No eye contact with the teacher because I did not want to read aloud
To prevent the students from laughing at me
Just waiting for the bell to ring
Could not ride a bike or skate or even swim
Use my height to walk in the pool
Quit learning to ride a bike or skate because
I fell so many times
As my confidence eroded
I would put myself down

Yet I learned how to drive a car
I will be learning how to swim
Ride a bike
Skate

I will ride in a hot air balloon
To overcome my fear of heights
Seek to rise above my fears
No longer hiding incognito
Living unapologetically
Not hiding but seeking greatness

Makayla (The Intro)
Davion Moore

I bet you won't make it
A boy said confidently
It is a hot Summer day
The sun beams down
Young kids are at play
While the older kids
Congregate on the basketball court
The boy who had just finished a game
Notices a girl shooting by herself
He decides to tease her
You sure about that? she says
He flashes a wide grin
He looks confident and has a strong feeling
He is right
She calls for the ball
Looks at the boy
Smirks and shrugs
And lets it fly
Swish!
Too easy, she says
The boy is stunned
All he can say is
I bet you don't make another

Sigh
She dribbles the ball and takes a step back
Lets it fly again
Swish!
The boy looks annoyed
Let's make it five, he says
She steps back yet again
A crowd starts to gather around
She smiles and shakes her head

Swish
Swish
Swish
She keeps knocking them down
The boy looks embarrassed
As people start to laugh
Lucky shots, he says
She dribbles towards him
Spins the ball on her finger
What?
You trying to play me one on one?
Maybe tomorrow, he says, walking away
Ohhhh
The crowd jeers
As he keeps walking

She can shoot, one kid says
What's your name?
Makayla, she says

Child's Play

Willie June Landers

A regular afterschool sunny day
Me and Suzy always went out to play
Not concerned 'bout the world and the hassle
We would run, skip, jump, and sometimes wrestle

Landed on her as she went tumbling down
She looked at me with an indignant frown
The air filled with a contentious notion
Don't do that again without emotion

We played like that over thousands of times
Same as jump rope, tag and nursery rhymes
Suzy is no longer that kind of friend
Innocent mindset now at screeching end

I'm immature and blindly could not see
Suzy got there long before stupid me
After getting up from the dirt and filth
I began to feel a burdensome guilt

This ominous atmosphere woke my senses
Any closer meant some consequences
What should I not do? Where should I not go?
As for right now, I simply do not know!

My Brother Got Me a Gold Chain

Tichina Ward-Pratt

I was a tomboy in 5th grade.
The style I most aligned with:
oversized jeans, white or black
large t-shirt, snapback with a team on it.

It was armor for the boy who was shot
and killed up the street from our house.
At the time, the only armor I knew
that offered immediate belonging.

I just wanted to play basketball not in a skirt,
wanted to fit in, in a way that said
I could also fall to the ground,
become completely filthy, and not blink an eye—

Mostly in anticipation of that rebound:
Box out,
get out of my way,
put back, and
off the backboard.
Yes, you got scored on by a girl!
Lift your head up, champ.

Later that year, I decided to get cornrows.
My Nana looked at me.
But not really at me,
at what she'd thought I'd become.
Told me I looked like a boy
and other things I can't remember.
Maybe she was disappointed.

In 6th grade, I never wore pants
that didn't fit tight,
or hats of any kind,
or oversized t-shirts.

Maybe I found new armor,
maybe I was finding myself,
maybe disappointment was
enough to keep me in a shell.

Years later, my brother bought
me a gold chain for Christmas;
a missing object in a time capsule
buried by a 10-year-old me.

Bike Race

Michael Kim Roos

It's been agreed indeed decreed among the three—
Ranger, Bailey, Stent—
The Inaugural Lynwood Bicycle Road Race Championship
shall begin promptly at whatevertimeitis
anywaysoon…rightabout…now
eggboil afternoon
17 August 1960
Cosmic Clock shouts, Riders up!

Ranger straddles
new-old Western Flyer whitewalls
Rocks back…forth…back…forth…
Snaps pinksquare baseball gum
Yankee Cap, Red Ball Jets.

Stent spits
flatblack Schwinn.
black hat, goth tee, U.S. Keds
tough Detroit kid
grunts, "What we waitin for?"
Spits again
"Just stay outa the way, bonehead."

Bailey on magenta junior bike
no fixed maker origin.
Green eyes dart leftright—
lime green shirt, purple socks, redwhiteblue Capri pants.
Stent scoffs, "Where ya get them baby pants?"

Riders forwardlean
"Mark!…Set!…Go!"
Straight up Shining Hill
Ranger wheelinfront
Stent wheelinfront,
Bailey trailing

Turn Two
Ranger-Stent wheeltowheel
Glanceback
Bailey slowing
too much Shining Hill
Ranger headdown pumppump
Stent cominthrough
Hairpin
Brakin nobrakin!
Danger! Ranger!
Rubbermetal violent silence
floating in a seaofsoup.
Cosmic Clock stops
Is this…Death?
Faraway galaxies implode
Underwater publicpool
Stent and Bailey float over
"Cool shit! Can't ya brake? Back-pedal, man!"
Crumpled Flyer,
youngblood tongueblood
Clouds under trees
"He's okay."
"He don't look okay."
Ranger sings. "Red…red…bob…dob…hobbin."
 "Blood, man. Cool shit."
"Leave him alone. Ain't gonna die."
"Anyways, I win. Race over."
Ranger feels Yankeecap.
Crap! Billcrushed
No, no. Yogi says, "ain't over—
Till it's—" what?
Wander wobblebike home.
Where? Over there.
Underwhere.
No, yes, no,
Ain't over, Stent, no over.

Solitaire

Julia Mallory

Wrists tilted
Fingertips determined
She evicts
The cards from the deck
By threes
Trios of potential triumph
Grandma is teaching me
How to play solitaire
An exercise in loneliness
Sometimes
I win

The YMCA saves my son's life maybe I am being overly dramatic

Gia Civerolo

Short-handed, the Latina ladies come get me,
my son is too much for them that day
I cry, they hug me, pray for me on the spot
Tell me it will be OK. I don't believe them that day.
In the end they were right.

Basketball teaches my son
his social skills, discipline
how to be respectful on and off the court
Plus, my boy be ballin'!
But high school dashes NBA dreams
with paid school coaches
not half as good as the volunteers at the Y
He's fifteen when he quits
doesn't want his Mama in his head
I am worried when I run into his old coach and cry
The next day he has my son running drills
Coaching little kids to their own basketball glory
In action he learns to give back
to a community that always let his light shine
Something my words just could not do

Baton Lessons

Pam Ward

I took two baton lessons and quit
leaving the metal rod
next to the ice skates and bike
I'd already abandoned for good.
It wasn't until Leslie
moved next door that I used it again.
Leslie liked to talk shit
popping her gum in my face
splattering her slobber on my neck.
But one day I snapped
ran home and grabbed my baton
put on my pink tights, glitter top
walked back outside
and whooped her right there on the sidewalk.
I remember gripping it
exactly the way I'd seen Willie Mays
then twirling like in a parade.
Mom made me apologize that time
dragging me down to their house
lecturing about stones & sticks
but secretly I was proud
she'd gotten me those lessons
you never know which tricks
come in handy.

Field of Dreams
Pam Concepcion

I walk towards a box
of white chalk, lined
on freshly watered soil.

The soles of my feet
feel the heat
from beneath
as I slide my cleats
from left to right
until common ground
is found between the two.

Through squinted eyes
and rusted grills
I look past the ground
beyond my box
and lock my gaze
on the mound across.

As throws wound up,
pings and dings and thuds
echoed in the box
Creating a beat
leading to a chorus
from a distance
I hear cheers and jeers
yet my mind remains
distant
from the refrain
when my fears
are at such a close distance.

So I shifted my stance
to follow the pace
of the pacing rhythm

hoping to get on base—
bracing for the throw that
throws off my rhythm.

Within two hundred fifty feet
from where my feet stand,
are the stands where
game-winning hits often land
on someone's bare hands.

As I fix my stance in the box, I pray
that today is the day
I finally reach the stands.

Basketball Love

James Coats

Basketball was my first love as a kid
Played on for hours with my best friends
Pure joy sweating and dripping from our faces
Summer afternoons until the Sun hit the bench.

We practiced "junior junior sky hooks" like Magic's
Shot that beat the Celtics on national TV,
Had no endorsement deals for shoes we wore,
Had this game, dreams, and memories worth millions.

we learn to win using someone else's moves

Cory Cofer

We two-on-two
On cleft asphalt
Under a smiling sun

Somebody's uncle
From two duplexes down
Ganders at smiling sons

With skinny, black, wailing arms
three-two-one-ing

Last-minute shots

Toward a rickety backboard
Of less screws

Under a cloudy sky
Of less blue

Through the legs
Around the back
Up and under

Magic
Jordan
Dominique
Kareem

This is how we dream

Dribble

Marlana-Patrice Pugh Hamer

For Bro Wiley

Not sure why they say only male fireflies can fly. Still, fly.
Must be the physics of height and velocity.
Some men contemplate free throws in their sleep,
peak performances conditioned during embryonic stages.

Some women were once talented tomboys.
Girls, never heralded for Greatness.
Not with those names!
King James. Air Jordan. Black Mamba.
The Answer. The Truth.

Once upon a time, the pavements met our knees.
Scraped them. Consecrated them.
We got up for **Cocoa Butter** glories.
Bouncing so high, we touched maple-tree limbs.
Dunking over our baby brothers
and their friends.

Gurlz and Boyz
under streetlights together,
sometimes falling down.
Traveling.
Talking is **Treasure.** Not **Trash.**
Laughing about games.
Taking turns at free throws.
Respecting everyone's lanes.
Shooting hoops.
Hitting rims of hopes.
For Boyz and for Gurlz.

Frogman Swimming Lessons at George Washington Carver Park

Ron Dowell

At 15, I learned to swim
the hard way as July's sun
blazed, keen on my skin ash.
There was nothing official

like weekly prepaid lessons
from former Olympians,
like a heated indoor pool;
On our own, we were tadpoles
in a chlorinated concrete tub.

                 Chlorine
        to murder spit,
    body oils,

and cousin Pookie's piss,
a reckless killer. I gulped
shallow water, preened
in Sea Green gym trunks.

I learned to swim when Glen,
my best friend, pushed and said,

Face down,
      spread your arms,
          just don't breathe,

of course. *Float,* he said, *kick.*

My nostrils burned, and my eyes
turned cranberry once, I observed,
I could see while submerged

in the over-chlorinated
Carver public park pool,
underwater, a Navy frogman
scuba diving like Lloyd Bridges.

Chlorine sanitized, searched
and destroyed insects and shit.
Deeper and deeper, I clung
along the pool drain edges,
tippy-toed, water to my chin,
I splashed wild-eyed when bully-
bumped

                into deep water,
        where tight-lipped, Chlorine-
    shocked liquid made no trespass.

I am a toad that learned
to Vaseline away the ash,
and survive chlorine's sting.

GAMES OF LIFE

Rock Hard

Sutichai Savathasuk

Sweat
Dripping
Off
Skin
On
Hard
Body…
You rope me in
with thrusting hips
rubbing off one another,
fine jugs I firmly grasp.

You arch your back with
a rigid crack I slip my meat in;
fists, twists, sticks my feel in,
upright and erect.
Dived deep into that cleavage
tight with forearms.

With a curvature to caress
these slopes, I flashed you.
You're a mountain to mount,
a hill to climb.
I'd need trimmed fingernails
to finger that hole.

Your figure ate mine but not before
a tradition to believe another round
I'd need to dip and lather my hands
in that slicky, white substance.

To care, I've been there.
To harness raw power,
that's dy-no-mite.
I'm getting bolder.

And when I've reached climax…
I crash onto pad.

I do love
rock climbing.

You Make Love Like a Pinball Machine
Cynthia Allesandra Briano

The focus, the rolling of silver, the   lopsided bunt,
Love, it is not   the thumbed jab of the lever
that keeps   the mercury rolling, nor

the spasmkick of knee
That retrieves those lost balls, still

I ring my encouragement, ring
'cause it doesn't even matter that I'm
always   kinda   off to the side

a slanted   amusement device
you roll down   with a   bump
Even when   all your springs are exhausted, I

whirr and   blink at the
score I pretend not to keep

the it'll do buzz
the little-point pong

the spiral
spring of laughter
and

woop
at the

occasional

thousand-point

ping.

52 Pick-Up

Aiyana Sha'niel

When you hear, "It's complicated,"
It doesn't mean that it's hard for me to explain
If anything I'm stopping myself from being too open
It's complicated because
I can't read your thoughts so
I'm not willing to share mine and
Risk another shot hit my soul
I'll tell you "It's complicated"
As a shield for myself
To not be vulnerable
Let you see my guard be broken
I'll tell a half-lie
And convince you it's more complex than it actually is
Because in reality
I could put it clear as day
Questions too close for comfort
Things are only complicated because I know
Exactly what I want for once
I juggle between speaking from the heart
And not being a plain fool
I don't want to lose my sense of royalty
In your eyes
It's only complicated because
I suck at playing games
So I can't tell when to hold 'em, fold 'em, or throw the pile away
Yes I'm shuffling the deck because this part isn't what's complicated
I don't know how to verbally play my hand
Even when it's the clearest thing on the table
So sorry
I will claim complication
To avoid explanation, not because it's intricate or elaborate
But simply because if it means you are quitting after I speak
I would rather keep my cards to myself

The Nike Narcissist

Woodrow Bailey

This sunny September in 1979
was the real LA time
I could finally find

I was able to shop for my own clothes
new colors, patterns with some goals

My parents still had say-so, money and control

Early on a bus trip before school
my buddy and I thought it would be cool
To go to the mall to try to act a fool

We walked around being complete frauds
looking for acceptance with applause

Remember we had no money or credit cards

As we traveled, we tried to be someone else
with a typical shirt, pants and belt
Now we know how everyone else felt

The mall of Fox Hills was not that old
all the air conditioning made it seem cold

It's designed for those with money to hold

Suddenly, in a grown-up shoe store
I couldn't ask for fake anymore
Never seen a shoe like that before

Some crisp clean white leather
making that design that much better

Plus, a black swooshing emblem was clever

I was now hypnotized
my buddy was surprised
We both fantasized
I wasn't self-centered with personality you see
my motive was to be different or extreme

These new kicks will get the best of me

I cannot stick to my parents' script
those gems would make me legit
I have come too far to pretend to quit

I ask the salesman "How much?"
I was hoping for some green luck

"$37.99 with tax, young Buck"

I already knew what my Pop would say
"Boy you better be playing in the NBA."
need to figure out a plan that pays

I thought about selling some of my comic books
the stage was set for all the good looks

Had to careful of those cheating crooks

Infatuation was now my destiny
admiration couldn't be easy
I'll be ruthless and save my lunch money

Easier said with hungry breath than done
40 days of starving is how it's done

My desire will rise as the dawning sun

I survived on candy, charity with hope
that grumbling stomach was no joke
All for a cause to learn how to cope

The time that pressed a dollar a day
no one will stop my shoe parade

I praised myself on the 40th day

I walked into the living room to show Pop
"Can you take me to the mall so I can shop?"

"Boy what the Hell you talking about?"

I showed him 40 George Washingtons,
savings without committing a sin

A rare 16-year-old is going for the win

Pop glared at my newfound cashflow
he slowly got up and said "Let's go."
I was going to be the star of this show

West on Slauson the south on Bristol
start saluting the newest show hero

Persevered to gain kicks control
I bounced through the mall into the shoe store
Salesman laughed at my smile with style galore
"Men's size 10 with a black swoosh, Mr. Royal."

The silky soft white leather cradled my feet
they danced and shout without being discrete

Pop said get a box and a receipt

Morning hurry up so can get to Dorsey High
for once I will walk in with pride
I rolled in with a float as they flew by

All the Ballers want to walk up on my pick
I yelled not to walk up on my clean kicks

Nobody could get a close look with their tricks
That's when the Nike swoosh captured me
This notion was placed in my psyche
The time was my "Just Do It" destiny

Nearly 45 years swoosh-wearing years later
Nothing can compare or be greater

Then getting Nike swag as I love all the flavors

I lost count on how much I have
shirts
shorts
socks
shoes
sweat suits with duffle bags

My son is a legacy to the swoosh
worked at a Jordan store to boot
hard to argue with this truth

My grandson will wear them too
another legacy will be really cool

Always being complimented with approval

Simplistic
Socially accepted
Is the Nike Narcissist

A Dream Lost in a Day

Marilyn 'Quinoaa' Wilson Hamasu

Happy
She ran across the open fields of Mississippi like a barefoot Cheetah

Strong
She ran through the streets of Detroit, like a stallion set loose for the first time

Confident
Top runner in her track and field class

Proud
They called her speedy

Free
She ran so fast she looked like she was flying

Dream
Catch Wilma Rudolph

Until
The day her wings were clipped, and she did a free fall back to Earth

Day of the Antithesis
Slipped capital femoral epiphysis

Pain and Sorrow
Her lifeless limbs dangled from their sockets

Crippled
Her only tools; wheelchairs and handicapped schools

Time lost
Learning to walk again

Too Late
Too late to catch Wilma Rudolph

No world Stage
Only tragedy at a young age

A dream lost in a day

She dances

Philosophy

For my niece Princess Alyssa T

She dances…
as thunder erupting
in the cloud cover,
as lightning,
restricted in its ability to be seen,
and yet,
cracking the night sky
with its brilliance,
illuminating the world
with every bolt, spearheaded,
or hurled towards Earth.
She dances,
as footprints emerge from concrete,
cementing her choreography in history,
be it Julliard,
or her footsteps,
in the yard of the White House,
weathering the storms,
as ballet shoes plié
toward the jazz of the Earth's core.
unearthing the plate tectonics
and shifting the landscape
of hip-hop beneath her feet.

Indiscreetly she dances,
cuticles closed in her palm
with a tight clasp on her success,
with every rehearsal.
grasping at her fingertips
and extending arms,
to reach her goals.
She dances,
Spirit forward, tenacious,
and fearless,

in the direction of her truth.
Excellence is a byproduct
of hard work.
Losing isn't an option.
when winning
courses-through your veins.

Dancing is not a hobby.
It is life!
and blood pumps through her heart
for this moment, second,
or light year on stage.
She is infinite as space and time,
and thrives for every inch
of this square space
to express herself,
in this art of dance,
with her artistry answering,
the calling of her purpose.
So she dances,
As if God peeled back
the cumulus cloud,
and peered down from heaven,
with a copper-colored telescope
in search of radiance,
and those using their talents
for the greater good of humanity
and looking toward a lighthouse.
Shedding light,
as philanthropist sharing wealth
to heal nations
with the softness of giving

Thus she gives all she has in sacrifice
of the Craft...
"SERVANT... WELL... DONE..."
Heard by adolescent ears,
while small hands lace up ballet shoes,

and begins to practice
again and again
rehearsing routines
Again
She dances as a mirror image,
in reflection of God's gift on Earth,
bestowed for all humans
to behold her majesty.

Happy

Eric DeVaughnn

I heard a leaf skittering across the ground carried along the gutter by water flowing from someone washing a car farther up the street

So, I raced to see which leaf had called to me. Watched her scuttle past, dragging her stem amidst the burbling of an impromptu stream

a curious thing so happily alive and out of place.

I sat on the curb, dropped more leaves to sail, laughed at the soapy suds collecting at the tire

of my girlfriend's truck. This all felt familiar, like

seven years old, long before technology moved our play indoors, when trees and water and wind were still enough to entertain a child for hours..

I think it was this spirit of play cautioning me

to take time from my adult frustrations and stress, reminding me that I was once and maybe still am happy.

I rushed inside to write this poem and my Love asked me to come out back to see the sky. I began to describe this

beauty, the wonder of reliving a childhood joy and they

walked away to snap a picture of the view. And I waited to see if she would remember that I'd been talking at all.

Now I sit again on this curb, writing this poem, and wonder how we ever manage happy endings or was it always so

simple as deciding where the story stops

Baseball Gophers in the Palm Lane Public Housing Projects

Ron Dowell

We weren't allowed hamsters, dogs, or cats,
So, we spent our summers playing baseball,
We set aside our prey on mice and black rats.

We played each morning to starry nightfall,
Flashing, we'd swoop and flit like butterflies,
Summer assured us we'd hear umpire calls.

At year nine, a power bat I'd wield with pride
On gopher-holed infields and ankle sprains,
Clip-winged viceroys, we stole bases pie-eyed.

My goal was to shortstop with skill and brain
Until a ball caromed off a gopher's head
And struck hard my throat, which I grabbed in pain.

I moved to center field and did not wane,
I dabbed at tears but stayed in the game.

we hit homeruns on accident, while learning to swing for the fences

Cory Cofer

We swing for the stars
We swing to be stars

We swing dismembered branches
At orphaned tennis balls

And sprint to old garments
And trashbags
Disguised as bases

We run for the races
Until we reach home

We throw, we slide, we hit
In school pants
and playshoes

We fit thrift-store mitts
Over dirty palms, no quit

And learn to squeeze until
Until we learn to catch

Rickey Henderson
Doc Gooden
Reggie Jackson

This is how we dream

Losing Cousins

Evan Gore

It is not just you
Leaping outstretched to grab history
On the fly
To connect with the instant
That will freeze a man into bronze
Like some kind of war hero
Like some kind of baseball metaphor
As your heart punches through your jersey
Because for complicated reasons
You care what jersey you wear
When you spring up
Dropping your brat in disbelief,
Electrified with hope and elation
Over a kids game played by elites
Trying to get into history books
Like you
Yearning for this moment to
Become what we used to call
A magazine cover
A perfect, permanent memory.
It is not just you.
It is mostly me.

When we were just about to
When we almost
When we came so close
When we deserved to
When we wanted it more than
When we thought we were going to
Stand so tall
Scream so loud
High-five strangers
Swearing we saw this coming
Believing we deserved this greatness
Knowing we would float above them

Remembering we were losers
Losers for years
My guys, the guys on my mind
The guys I have worried about
Whose histories I learned like mythology
Whose cheering parents
Put a lump in my throat
Whose toddlers made me click share
My emotional cousins, adopted on faith
My cousins fucked up. They fucked it up.
My guys dropped the ball and me
They dropped my family.
They embarrassed themselves and me
And I feel sorry for them and me
My sad little cousins
Trying to be important
So I could be important
Trying to express their excellence
Making a goose egg of shit.
These human individuals
These disappointing heroes
With their surgery-bound elbows and
Twisted tendons, their soft tissue
And breakable kneecaps
Following their love
For us, for that moment
For their ambition for their moms
Just like you but more like me
When they worked together
After laughing and dancing
When their bats pulverized
When their throws pin pointed
And everyone believed
Their gloves were dipped in gold.
Its not just you, baseball
Breaks my heart too.

Silver and Black 2.0

Molimau Andrew Fatu

Surrender is never an option
For we are Raider Nation
Ready to lead our people to
Victory by all means,
Not just on the football field, but in life with the
Commitment to excellence as our goal
Revolutionaries who are anti-establishment
With a never-say-die attitude
Dominating all those who come in our way
Boldly, with our voices and actions loud
Heard all over the world and beyond
Anticipating the rise of the underdogs,
Those forgotten and underestimated,
Those who never got the chance to shine
For now it is that time to kick open the doors

We have been waiting forever and
Have put in the work and
Now it is our time to
Just win, baby
Regain our roar and rise
For we are divine beings with an attitude
Who will ignite the flame and
Carry the torch to brighten within us all

We will see our people living for
Eternity in excellence
Reminding the world of
Our ancestral greatness and our
Soular power to shine
Through our hard work, adversity, poised for winning
Wearing silver and black walking proudly
Raising our fists and football helmets
Yelling Raaaaaaaaaaaiiiiiiiiiidddddddeeeeeeeeerrrrrrrrrrssssssssss

Moving and Going

Saint Ice

In loving Memory of Mr. William Crain

I know a Mr. William
Seasoned senior citizen
Energetic, enigmatic, six-foot plus
Always moving, always going

Long locks and curious curls
Formulate white mane and beard
Gift for script and story
Net worth near millions
Always moving, always going

Through the Sunset skyline window
We see a scurrying squirrel
He has named Paul Bunyan
I smile as he shares with me
And the squirrel
His encounters with the world.
In traveling tongue and grey glaring eyes
I catch a glimmer of his summers
As an open water swimmer
And a long-distance runner

Now his slender form braced
Against his walker, voice softer
Pushing for laps around his living room
Summoning legs to movement
Has become his workout, though not by choice

Mr. William and his doctor swap stories
About their sons playing ball
Lil' Will with a bat, in his cleats standing six feet tall
The doc, proud poppa, exclaims
His boy shares a court with son of King James.
Tells Mr. William to pick up his pace.
He has to eat better to stay in the race

Our visit completed, the seasoned citizen leaves slowly
Talking softly, walking softer into the sunset of his glory

Long locks and curious curls
Formulate his white mane and beard
A mileage-manifested creative soul
Always moving, always going

Back Down Memory Lane
AKoldPiece

Walk with me
Back down Memory Lane
Back to the games we played
Before the digital age
Remember—
Eeny meeny miney moe
Catch a tiger by his toe
If he holla let him go
And—
Bubble gum, bubble gum in the dish
How many pieces do you wish?
Back when—
Boys wanted to be Bruce Lee
And made ninja stars out of paper
And went around kickin' karate
Waaaa-taaaa!
Whatever happened to slapjack?
Slapping food out of each other's hands
25-cent grab bags from the ice cream truck
(Where dem donuts come from?)
We slap boxed
And it always turned into a real fight

Back then you knew who gang bang
Nowadays thugs look different
In little t-shirts and skinny jeans with leopard print
Aye, where you from?
I laugh
Cannot take him serious 'cause
I know he got his outfit at Forever 21

I wanna go back to a time that was fun
Back when I was young
Back when we would watch the girls
Like they were putting on a show!

Jig-A-Lo, Jig, Jig-A-Lo
My hands are high, my feet down low
And that's the way I Jig-a-lo
And—
Ms. Mary Mack Mack Mack
All dress in black black black
With silver buttons buttons buttons
All down her back back back!
When—
We played hide-and-go-seek
Football in the street
Sideline pop!
Basketball in the backyard
Byron Scott jumpshot!
Kickball with baby bouncies
Racing to the water hose
Eastside kids knew
When you take off your shoes you run faster
If you took too long someone started counting
I'm thirsty!
You gotta be quicker than that!

Saturday morning cartoons
Soul Train that afternoon
Ooh, that's why I'm easy
I'm easy like Sunday morning
Whatchu know 'bout
Poppin & Lockin
The Robot, the Robocop and The Whop?
Can't forget about the Electric Side and the Butterfly
Oh oh oh oh that's old
Let me see the tootsie roll
And for my reggae folks
Killing with it, killing with it,
killing with it, killing with it,
Heads high, kill dem wit it now
Back then—
Lunch time dances in the Girls Gym

Y'all red light parties in the basement
Most girls were and most boys lied
About being a virgin
(I heard some stories)
When kids could be kids
And
One-two-three NOT IT!
started a game

We looked forward to summer break
You could go outside and play all day
And you knew you had to be home
Before the street lights came on

Skate Girl

Carlton The Messenger

She was in the back of the skating rink
Soft drink and some fries
rolling her eyes at the guys
trying to relate and skate with her

That wouldn't detour me
I was on my way to her
I knew what to say to her for her to choose this
I stepped up
She like, Who's this?
I said, Messenger's my name
and I'd like to take you for a ride on your urethanes
on the oak, entertain you acrobatically systematically
in this building self-contained
Tune your channel to my vibe, Yeah!
Involve you in a revolving circular rhythmic path,

She asks, Who talks like that?
You got a mental condition?
I laughed
You ain't met a brother who knows how to
collate the vapors of human experience
into a viable and logical comprehension
She say, Naw I can't say that I have

You wanna skate? that's what I was saying with this
She said, That what was buried in all that craziness?
But don't wanna fall, she grins
Who you playing with? I aint gonna wreck the Benz
Ain't like you one them Toyotas I be skating with
I am a top-flight skater of the world,
not the city, not the state, but the world
and Ima woo you on these wheels
I got skills that amuse
I'm the reason some fool put wheels on shoes

Just hold on tight, we gonna be all right
Plus you seat cushion can be used as a flotation device
She smiled as she looked back at me
with them lips that would make a lollypop happy
We fell into the groove, my moves were right
and we let the DJ spin our night

I found she was from out of town
so what goes down can't be taken too seriously
but she was curious of me
Invited me to her room for drinks
She wanted to experience me, I was guessing
She ask if I was ready for a honeymoon salad
I said, Whats that?
She said, Lettuce alone, no dressing

Shallow

Carole Leila Cramer

The striped line of demarcation
that indicates the
deepening of the pool,
from safety to danger
taught me well.

Needing to feel things out to feel safe,
I became afraid and overwhelmed
if I could not feel my feet touching the bottom

Not learning how to swim until I was 18
was a great hindrance in my life,
both above and below ground.

Because of it
I learned early on that there are some lines
that are not to be crossed-
in the pool and in real life.

Neither line should be crossed
if you're not prepared to deal with
the consequences of diving deep.
As long as I tip-toed in the shallow end,
I did not have to worry about the danger
to my physical self.

In real life,
it's the unleashing of strong emotions
we don't know how to handle.
As long as I only skimmed the surface,
I did not have to worry about exposing those dangerous
feelings that I'd buried in the deep end
because of their danger to my emotional health.

Diving deep wasn't something that I could handle.
I did not learn how to do

an in-depth examination of my
submerged feelings until
a cathartic life-changing event.

Because of this,
fear of the water and drowning dominated my
thoughts.

Life really has a funny way of
bringing,
up and out,
all the emotions
that have previously been laid away
until we could afford them.

Ironically,
even though I stayed on the shallow side,
I was still drowning.

Run, Tomboy, Run.

Ravina Wadhwani

First there was the separation
womb to world in the span of a second,
A shriek and cry, loss of my first home
and breathing into a new life

Then there were the couple of falls
just to get back up when I learned my own balance.
Falling more times than the rise
was the only way to learn to walk
All I needed to get from point A to B
was my own two feet and a will to keep going

Hurricane Marilyn happened when I was three.
I was taught that all I needed to survive
when the world outside was destroyed, ravaged,
and uneasy to recognize was one candle,
and my father's voice to navigate through the darkness.

The basketball court was the first place
where I learned survival.

I had to sweat, run, jump, push my limits,
earn my chance to be seen among the boys around me,
had to prove that I was something to be chosen,
grappling with those who I loved who took up too much space.

But boy could I chase them down the block if I had to.
Thick skin formed from the jump.
How I could still catch my breath when challenged,
broken down, bruised, beaten, yet body still alive.

On the court I wiped my tears on my own,
used my own fingers to rub honey into the wounds of bee stings,

fended for my own damn self,
learned not to take shit from anyone
who grabbed the ball from my hands,
snatched it right back strategically

Being the only girl among the boys wasn't a hard thing,
just a constant lesson. My rough edges born from the fight,
from the struggle.
because being the youngest little girl among all of them
meant learning from boys and thinking like them too.

A constant run flip and jump to get to the top
A continuous chase of claiming my seat at the table.
Shooting a shot for what I wanted and needed.
A dribble and a pass, a rebound from the fight.
A game I have mastered no matter the scraped knees, cuts and bruises.

Watch me as I run past, to claim what I deserve,
to grasp onto what was meant to be in my hands.

Chiefly Tennis
LaCole Foots

It's the back and forth
The thrill of the court
Chasing for sport
Overcoming our nerves
Our best we serve
Set ourselves up to score
The paradox of the pursuit
Is we have to be delicate
In each step we choose
It makes sense, don't it?
You can lose love at any moment
especially when you
slam on your opponent

Taking the Tennis Bus

Mark Gozonsky

I took the following notes to share this long, long bus ride's sensation of
everlasting foreverhood:
Sunset Boulevard twisty, turny
Sepulveda as 405 side street
San Fernando Valley panorama peek-a-boo
passing bus stops I've stopped or waited at
auto row in Sherman Oaks
ugliness
grotesquerie
monotony
mortuary next to bail bonds
express bus lane hurtling
sycamore trees
pine trees
I don't know trees
trucks in camo at Woodley and Victory
barbed wire
open fields
baseball fields
backyard garages
jacaranda finally in bloom
more sycamore
fake adobe
real adobe
dispensary
Burrito El Chivo
Reseda in the Tom Petty song "Free Fallin'"
cypress tree
pepper tree
pool cleaner's extra-long squeegee
gray-hoodie'd rider on azure bicycle
encampment tents
circus tents
Trophy Max
Canoga Park—THIS IS ME.

Team Player

Lester Graves Lennon

Bill Robinzine? Oh, man why you ask me?
That boy was just one crazy Son-of-a-Gun.
You never knew what he was gonna do.
Like the time Chocolate Thunder slammed the ball
over poor Bill so hard the backboard cracked
like a rifle shot, the glass explodin, rainin,
just pouring down, the players frozen, shocked.
Then BAM get outta here, save your ass, NOW.
There's Bill, you've seen the tape, he's hoppin, dancin,
runnin, arms over head and ears, like he's
heard somethin terrible, and tears, boy's sobbin.
Never seen nothin like it on the court.
Don't get me wrong, you wanted Robinzine
on your team; big-toothed barrel-chested horse
would work the boards, set picks, nice short-range jumper.
Team man, that's the key; he loved the team, felt needed.

But his knee, always the knee.
Folks were just gettin bigger like the money:
fresh corn-fed farm boys, fear-fed ghetto kids.
And Bill sure wasn't no Ice, no Silk; he had
to shove and bang the boys hard to survive.
Sad thing his leaving. Basketball was all.
You knew it would be rough alone. Those strange
doe eyes were way too big to hide his tender
insides. But this, so damn quick, suicide?
It made me think real fast of Chocolate's dunk
and Bill protectin his head, movin wild
like he just knows he hears that future shot,
and misses what he's runnin from so crazy
he's runnin to so hard.

Dad's Fourth Quarter Pass

Marlana-Patrice Pugh Hamer

Sitting near his wise wingback chair,
at home with Dad, football, and male codes.
Football Sunday in our family living room.
"What does a quarterback really do?"
"Patsy, just watch. Stop asking so many questions."
Dad expected me to learn mostly by watching.

Sometimes chairs are at bedsides.
Livid just looking at wall clocks.
Mocking me. Mocking us.
Forcing me to teleport one more time to a Browns game.
A win or lose Cleveland thing.

My latest reverie about winning playoff tickets just for Dad and me
halted momentarily while nice nurses take turns
coming in and out of our cuckoo clock.
The doctor, skilled clocksmith repairing in other rooms.
Finally arrives with Hope, nothing more.
Hospitals filled with only Hope make anyone ready for more morphine.

Hope sat in the room with us all day.
Then Dad's faltering breath kept telling her to go away.
Hope could not take away the gray air.
Hope could not take away his renal failure.
Hope could not stop Dad's prostate cancer from metastasizing.
Hope could not take away Dad, lying there still and silent
like he was already pronounced dead.
No longer able to even whisper my name.
Hope could not keep me from falling asleep
right before Dad died.
Yes, I cried, unable to say Goodbye
while he was at least somewhat alive.

Doctors say concerned fathers often slip away.
I imagine Dad sat in his chair one last time while his slow
breaths lulled me. Lullabied me to sleep right before.

Not surprised Dad needed to be Dad that afternoon.
Filling me with team spirit.
Enough to become our family's new quarterback.

LEGENDARY GAMES

Ollamaliztli [pronounced hola-ma-lease-tlee] (The Sacred Mesoamerican Ballgame)

Carlos Ornelas

Before the sacred game begins we ask consent from the four winds,
From the moon and the sun, the Aztec God Twins.
We ask permission before we enter into the Sacred Ball court.
This is Ollamaliztli, one of the world's oldest sports.
None enters from the crowd, only warriors allowed.
We ask permission from the four corners of the earth.
We ask for guidance from our ancestors, firm upon the dirt.

In ceremonial regalia, they have arrived,
Our five chosen players who will represent our tribe.
Headdress of jade and feathers, snake rattles tied to ankles.
Fingers buried in the mud are then streaked across the chest.
War paint is unformed upon the flesh to distinguish
from the rest. Thick leather band tied around the waist.
Ball made from rubber trees of the Mesoamerican plains.

The opposing tribe arrives with regalia of its own…
The depiction of our gods has been carved and etched in stone.
Two large hoops, 20 feet high, might as well be in the sky,
Hang above like sun and moon, one on each opposing side.
Just one shot will end the game, and the losers die in shame.
All the grounds adorned in red and if you lose, you lose your head.
Sacrificed inside the court, our three-thousand-year-old sport.

This is more than just tradition. It is part of our religion.
You can call it Pok-Ta-Pok. It's the world's deadliest sport.
And the player first to score may have just prevented war.
There is no mercy for the weak. Karma gives you a defeat.

If you cannot beat the odds, sacrifice you to the Gods.
And a victory is glory, may the elders tell our story.
How we played until our doom, and our blood made flowers bloom.
'Til invaders came and killed the empire we had built.
And our blood was spilled in vain. This is more than just a game.

It's the tale of our existence 'til they toppled our resistance.
All that remains are the ruins which prove we once occurred.
How we flourished for millennia, then we vanished from the earth.
But since death is temporary, it is time for our rebirth.

Wilt

Mike Bonifer

Had my first ten-foot hoop
Bright orange ring and white nylon net
Mounted on carpentered backboard
Bolted to a hickory pole
On the family farm in Indiana
Where basketball was religion
Where congregations gathered
On Friday and Saturday nights
To worship in glowing churches
Young gods in holy wars
Of zone and man-to-man
Fast break and pattern ball
Local legends fill these halls
Pete Gill. Jumpin' Jack Steinhart.
Junior Gee. Larry and Bugsy Humes. Dave Small.
Oscar. The Van Arsdales. Rick Mount.
I am them all
Pass me the ball

I shoot hoops in all seasons
When the net is frozen
And my bounce-less Voit will not drop through
When the grass has given up
And my court is muddy
And covered by cardboard in spring
Baked hard with tractor tracks in summer
That I wear away by fall.
Me and that basket and that ball
Morning, noon, night by yard light
Put the ball in the hoop
Shoot. Shoot. Shoot.

Never mind getting animals fed
Or homework done
Never mind getting ready for church

Or coming to supper when Mother calls
Put the ball in the hoop
Follow through like Coach taught me to
Shoot. Shoot. Shoot.

With each shot I move another step
Closer to the pantheon
Of gods who fly ball to basket
On Friday and Saturday nights
While people scream their names
And reverence their game with passion
They don't give to Jesus Christ

Who I most want to be is Wilt Chamberlain
Of the Philadelphia Seventy-Sixers
Wilt the Stilt. The Big Dipper.
Who plays his games on Sunday
Like the major gods do

The object of my mania
Once scored a hundred points
Against the New York Knicks
In a game played in Hershey, Pennsylvania
A hundred points! These high school boys
These Wildcats, Spuds and Yellowjackets
Do well to go for eighteen or twenty
Wilt went for a hundy
That. That's me. That's who I want to be.

Thirteen, that's our number
Me and Wilt say fuck your luck
We'll make our own
I wear a rubber band on my left wrist like Wilt does
To call attention to the fact
That Wilt and me are not our jewelry
One day I'll wear knee pads *below* my knees like Wilt
To call attention to the fact
That your puny ass will never

Live up to our majesty
Shoot. Shoot. Shoot.

Shoot like Wilt shot the ball that night in Hershey
When he, a historically pathetic shooter of the freebie
Because Wilt does not take charity
Sinks twenty-eight of thirty-two from the stripe
Proving that when Wilt and me put our minds to it
Ain't nothin' we can't do
Bank the ball through the hoop
Shoot. Shoot. Shoot.

For a player as big and powerful as I
I am remarkably humble
Help old ladies into hotel elevators
My tips put smiles on the faces of waiters
With grown-ups I'm aloof
With children kind
I drink half a gallon of milk at halftime
My fall-away shot cannot be blocked
I may go for a hundred and twenty this time
Watch me put the ball in the hoop
Scream my name
Shoot. Shoot. Shoot.

Comes a day I realize that my chances of being
Seven-foot-one and spending a year
With the Globetrotters like Wilt are nil
The only way I'll dunk like the Dipper
Is by standing on the steps of a ladder
That is not Wilt Chamberrlain's dad
Calling from the barn right now
To come and water the cows
I cannot even jump and touch the rim,
But that doesn't stop me
From wanting to be him
Wanting Hef and Quincy and Miles
As my L.A. pals

Building a house in the Hollywood Hills
With no right angles
In its architecture
Decorated with oversized furniture

And mind you, before my story's through
I fully intend
To bed ten thousand women
Like Wilt would do
Shoot.
Shoot.
Shoot.
Put the ball in the hoop.
Make my own luck.
Score a hundred.
Be Wilt Chamberlain.

The 100-Point Game

Tom Meschery

For Wilt Chamberlain (8/21/36–10/12/99)

A rookie in '61, I watched
Wilt score a century in one game
in Hershey, PA, with the smell
of chocolate floating through the air
and Zink, our announcer, crying out
with each point, Dipper, Dipper dunk.

That night through the fourth quarter
in that mad scramble for history
we all passed the ball the full length
of the court to Wilt, straight and high
into the dark around the rafters
and every time the Dipper skyed
he caught the ball and scored.

After the game, there was no TV,
no reporters, only Coach McGuire
in the quiet locker room tugging
at his gold cufflinks, pointing
at the Dipper as if he'd just discovered
a new constellation, reminding us
he'd predicted before the season started
Will would score 100 points.

Later on, on the bus driving back to Philly
I watched a farmer in a horse and buggy
trotting through the dark Amish countryside
following the brief light of his lantern home.

2020+1 Tokyo Olympics
Pam Concepcion

We had only ever streamed games
on Facebook Live, brought to us
by a player's phone
on limited mobile data.
A static wide shot of soil and grass
behind a grid of metal grills, silhouettes of players,
a tok!, clusters of moving pixels, static screams—
the ball is in play.
We hear exclusive bench cheers, jeers and chatters
coaches cursing out gods, saints, and sharks—
our in-game commentary
while we constantly comment
"Anong inning na?"
"Ano na score?"
"Sinong lamang?"

Now, in this fully-funded effort
to bring the sport back,
every action captured
in high resolution. Every position covered
by at least three cameras.
It is a revolution
to my eyes: revelations of the body
at the professional level—
each fielder's frame built
to fit their function.
Seeing the rotation
of the batter's hips, waist
twisting, and arms gripping,
connecting bat to ball;
the reaction of a third baseman
as she fields a hard hit by the powdery foul line,
a suave backhanded pick-n-throw to first;
The motion of a baserunner
stealing and sliding into second base
dusty sandy soil smoking up the screen;

The emotion of teammates cheering
each other up after an error;
and the mere reflection of bodies
that look like mine and my teammates'.

Unlike college "chicks" on local TV
those cheerleaders in skirts,
those flexible fearless flyers
contort limbs on a tier, then in the air;
or those volleyball girls
serving, setting, spiking—
rallying with cold-blooded composure
in their chest-tight sleeveless jerseys,
thigh-hugging short-shorts.
Cameramen focus
on bodies slender and petite,
tall, busty and leggy
faces barely sweaty
always TV type pretty
always a fast-selling, high-rating day
thanks to middle-aged dads, caught
on camera 2, intently watching
"the game."

Our coach tells us stories
of her trips to the Little League World Series
How All-Star American girls step up the plate,
Video and Photoready.
Hair up with red, white, and blue ribbons;
and full-face make-up:
foundation, lipstick, eyeshadow, eyeliner, mascara
never batting an eyelash
at another team's homerun.
We see our seniors bringing home
the newest Easton or Louisville bats,
Rawlings mitts and batting gloves,
Nike cleats, and jerseys designed
for Asia Pacific.

That league was our own Olympics—
our Field of Dreams now stored
in the equipment room
at the back of our minds
until today

It's our turn to step into the batter's TV box now
So we scale internet fences and IP addresses
to tune in every zoomed-in,
slow-mo instant replay
of a pitch; every bead of sweat,
every speck of dirt
on sunburnt skin. It's been
two years since I last threw a fastball
but I can feel the seams of the ball leave
my fingertips. My feet dragging
on dirt, recalling the heat
beneath my cleats, and my weight
transferring from left quad
to right toes, springing my body
into a windmill moving forward
into a new life off the field
cheering
from digital stands.

Scapegoat

Mike Bonifer

Best Night of My Life.
We were ahead in top of the eighth,
One out, one runner on base,
When Castillo fouled a pitch
High into the night sky,
Oh baby, here it came,
A comet sent by the baseball gods
Stamped with my name.

How can I not reach out to accept
A gift from the baseball gods?
I mean, what are the odds?
One in five hundred sixty-six
When you're in my seat,
Aisle four, Row eight, Seat one-thirteen,
I'm an accountant by trade,
I know these things.

I touched but did not catch the gift,
Diverted its flight away from Moises' mitt,
Now Moises is pissed!
Taking his cue, everyone is booing me
For doing what they would've done
if they were me,
After that, our heroes fell that night,
And I had to go into hiding.
Worst Night of My Life.

I am the reason, according to the media,
That a magic season presto'd tragically,
I am the goat who cursed a city,
Destroyer of a generation
Of "I was there" stories
Told by one thousand two hundred times
The number of people

Who were actually there
I know the numbers.
I'm an accountant, goddammit,
A number-lovin' CPA.

Why you lookin' at me like that?
And dumping beer on my head?
Why am I the villain in this story?
I didn't boot the ground ball at short
Later in the inning,
I didn't lose the game, bitch,
Wasn't on the mound giving up hits,
Why you making me
A receptacle for your misery?

I am not the reason
You didn't pass the bar exam,
Not the reason you got that DUI
Or that your kid got sick,
Or your dog ran away
Or your faucet's running dirty water,
I am not the high school teacher
Who made a pass at your daughter.

You don't know this about me,
I'm really good with numbers,
At measuring the difference
Between what's on the books
And what's in the bank,
I count. I keep track,
I know exactly what you owe me—
An apology.

You turned my name into the butt
Of seven thousand jokes
That spread like an oil spill
On a stagnant river already polluted
By your life's regrets,

Your plasticized illusions,
Your drowned sorrows,
And the wreckage of your sunken dreams.

I know the numbers
I'm an accountant, goddammit,
A number-lovin' CPA!
I know the difference between
What you do and what you say,
What I did is what you would've done
When I made the mistake
Of believing a ball was a gift of grace
And not the fall I was about to take.

My bad. I admitted it.
But my bad wasn't even a millionth
Of what you came at me with.
I know the numbers.
An apology is owed.
That's the principal,
The interest is your atonement.

How about you make us whole again
By healing wounds you inflict on a daily basis
With the fuckwaddery of your ways,
Like the world stole your ticket
To a lottery you weren't going to win anyway?
I know the odds, I totalize for a living,
In percentages I see fate—
To get a break, you give a break.

I know the numbers,
I'm an accountant, goddammit
A number-lovin' CPA!
An apology is owed,
And you can count on this,
There will be a day,
When one way or another,
You. Will. Pay.

Dodgers Back on Top

James Coats

Sitting here rocking the Pantone 294 Dodger blue.
Got the cap, the shoes, and jersey, too.
My favorite, Jackie Robinson number 42.
It's our time to bring a championship home to L.A.
32 years have been a long wait but today is our day.

We '80s babies recall greatness.
Smell of Dodger dogs and roaring stadium sound,
Days of Hershiser dominating the mound
while Gibson swings for the fences.
Tommy Lasorda's managing relentless.

Here we are again, our dream coming to life.
Kershaw inning after inning delivering strikes.
Bellinger hitting bombs into the stands
to a crowd of real and cardboard fans,
Betts stealing the show and the bases.
Feels unreal to see the players' smiling faces.

2020 World Series Champs has a nice ring
after all the struggle, masks and quarantine.
We felt down and out sometimes
Was a season even possible?
But we never stopped believing, until we won.
This chip means so much because of what we've overcome.
Blue Crew doing it all, 'cause that's how we ball.
I'm proud to bleed blue, through and through.
Los Angeles, this championship is for me and you.

My Girls

Frank Allocco

We were down by eleven with five thirty to go
Our team was proud at thirteen and oh
The odds were long, our team was cold
Deep down inside, I begged, "Please don't fold."

Their team was tough, big and strong
This entire game, they could do no wrong
But we kept coming at them, we never quit
And finally, our shooting began to hit

We were down by five with three-twenty to play
"Play harder, good defense!" was all I could say
Our conditioning paid off, their legs grew weary
And with nine seconds to play, our huddle was teary

As I knelt in the circle, there was screaming in the stands
I looked up at my girls, they were all holding hands
"Don't foul!" I cried, "Please pressure the ball!"
We sensed in our hearts, they were ready to fall

Back out to the court for one last free throw
We had outscored the giants thirteen to zero
We were champions again, look up at the score
But today we gained something worth much more

We have struggled, worked hard, and had some fun
But today was the day that we became one
I'll remember your effort, your hustle, your grit
And proud of the fact that this team never quit.

crossover

da boogie man

it's all about the crossover
the ability to dismantle defense
with intense indecipherable handle
freezin' suckas in motion with a head
and body fake/that makes competition
convulse and shake like an epileptic in
an earthquake/you let the chumps talk
bull/then cut 'em up like steak/
stutter step to the left/make 'em flinch
ignite to the right/drop 'em off at the top
of the key with directions to the bench/

headed toward the hole with a dropped shoulder
if you are a glacier in antarctica in the ice age
in an ice storm eating ice cream in ice water
you couldn't get any colder/little kids in the park
will be practicing way after dark hoping to be like you
when they get older

the dude you just shook
is grabbing his ankle trying save himself from
the embarrassment of looking like he just got
took by an invisible crook/fans in the stands are
stuck between trying to talk and look/so they cover
their mouths and just point at what you did/the announcer calling
the game says he must be anointed with the holy ghost/because
he got competition calling on GOD when he gets in the post/

here comes back side "d" you read it easier than a one-page
one-syllable one-word book/although the game is all in the wrist/
the highlight reel is filled with impossible assists that come from
a pass with no look/this is so simple it's funny/he doesn't see
your man cutting to the hole/so he covers you/dummy/
he just sold his car for gas money

from your hand the ball is released
slicker and sweeter than honey-coated grease
if there is art in movement/then this is a masterpiece/

the ball perfectly placed beside the rim/your man rising
like helium-filled steam/the prelude to the dunk begins/

...by two hands the ball is snatched/arms
expand/triggering a slight arch of the back/a
slight pause/then the body contracts/
puttin' it down harder than a james brown
track/did you see dat/did you see dat/that's
why people come to the park/to play here you need
more than skill/you need titanium will and a warrior's heart/

this about trash talkin', skywalkin', windmill, tomahawkin',
double-clutchin', finger-rollin', fadin'-away, explodin'
to the hole and punctuatin' your statements with soul and
fire that go up and beyond sport/letting everyone know
that if they didn't come here to play, there's no need
for them to step on the court/

this here
is determination in its rawest form/the
place where legends are made and stars
are born/from a crossover

An Ogalala Thought
Wyatt Underwood

he walked out into the day
and had the Oglala thought
"this is a good day to die"
it amused him
he was no longer a warrior
if he ever had been
no, that was nonsense
from the age of six
he had fought his father and the doctors
to be a boy, teenager, young man, man
he had a heart condition
and doctors advised him to live cautiously
he jumped ditches
climbed rock walls
dug a trench in the desert during the day
and when a cautious man might have bought a sedan
he bought a motorcycle
he rode one after another for forty years
one Harley after another for twenty of those
he took those motorcycles where a sane man would not
have
and survived
may have thrived
yes, in some way he had earned the right to declare
"this is a good day to die"
not that he meant to
but if Death came to him today
he could claim he'd lived well
as well as he might have
he could die without regret or complaint
inside, he smiled at the walls of his new home
and started listing what he might do that day

the mexican leagues

Cory Cofer

On a Saturday morning
when the sun hits
snooze, worn cleats
trample moist soil
on dying fields.
Somebody's *tía* pushes a
stroller full of
ham-and-lettuce tortas
wrapped in foil.
Una cincuenta!
Little boys and one girl
play U8 in Chivas jerseys.
Some with blue stripes,
some red—some with blue
shorts, some black. The
other team is bright orange
and pristine and matching.
Fathers shout *bien* and
vamanos and *golazo* when it
happens. Mommas sit in
folding chairs with
bottomless cup-holders and
dreams of Jalisco.
They sip horchata and
mimosas and decorate
their babies in somebody's
jersey. They let them
dribble off to the side
where the
soil is now firm—
until it's their turn.

Runaway Diesel 2003!

Darryl Lewis

Shaq, you seven-foot deserter!
Was it the money?
If it was the money, I could have written you a check!
Though it would have bounced
like your free throws off backboards and the side of the rim.
I wanted to hack-a-Shaq you myself!
Our Game 4 trophy placed on San Antonio's shelf.

We outpaced the Pacers.
No brotherly love for the Answer.
Dethroned the Kings,
yet you abdicated your position!

We could have won six more in a row
without even one of your free throws.
As you Basquiated the paint,
Robert Horry throwing up perfect rainbows,
landing in a three-point, perfect pot of gold.

Bro!

How could you and Kobe have had that much
of a clash of egos?

We knew you were the OG,
and Kobe was the rookie.
We could have smashed the leprechaun's dynasty
by way of San Antonio,
wreaked havoc in New Jersey.
Instead, the fans of the Los Angeles Lakers
were victims of
a runaway diesel.

A Father Remembers
Frank Allocco

I knew you were destined for greatness the first time I held you,
Rubbed you with all of my heart and whispered,
"I don't know what you'll grow up to be, but whatever you do always strive to
be the best." Your competitive fire was fueled at an early age in whiffle ball,
garage hoops, games of catch. Subtle words of encouragement, big brown
eyes watching your mentor's moves.

Memorizing every step, every flair, waiting for your time to shine.
Rides with dad alone, always listening to the lessons, silently assuming the
Torch of excellence, worn nobly by those who preceded you.

In a drafty junior college gym, a little fourth grade boy in an oversized green
and gold jersey with the number fourteen
barely visible above his ill fitting shorts
Steps to the foul line down two with no time left:
Blocking it all out, establishing the resistance to pressure that would become
your song. Leading them on, making them believe…
"Imagine being the kind of player that people would come from miles
around just to see you play." Years later, a tiny freshman steps out in the state
quarterfinals with no fear as Thousands get a slight glimpse of what was going
to come.
On a long, silent bus ride home, you felt your teammates pain and
Promised yourself, they'd never feel it again.

Practicing alone, the flame of challenge grows, its heat overpowers you as
All of the lessons begin to come together, making sense now as you realize
it's more than just a game. Endless hours of practice, summers away, the ball
becomes an extension of your hand.
The sounds of a snapping net lull you to sleep each night as
You count the days until your destiny can be fulfilled.
The morning birds of summer end their awakening tune and
Finally, after all the years of listening and preparing…it's your turn.
You make your mark instantly, 25 times in fact,
Recognition comes with individual honors earned..but something's missing.

And then, a year later, the endless outdoor courts, tiny grade school
gymnasiums, recreation centers and high school gyms give way to the
Oakland Coliseum where the greatest ply their trade. Beneath the glare of the
brightest of lights another "great one" emerges as
A loyal army of brothers band together to touch the stars.
I remember your tired, sweat soaked, sagging body, still quiet and confident,
Arms triumphantly raised, finally content in securing your place in history.
The madness of your forefathers becomes your passion too
As you get better and better, learning the little things,
Living the big things: Discipline, Love, Sacrifice and Leadership.

One last summer of preparation awaited you like an old friend but
Too swiftly the leaves turned to brown and drifted slowly to the ground
As you realized that the hastening passage of time had now become your
enemy. You are beckoned to the Coliseum for one last song,
Playing it as sweetly as you had in the past, then
On to Arco Arena for a final shot to dance with the gods one last time.
But this time, an exhausted, thoroughly used up
Braveheart from another era departed with one last kiss and embrace.
Standing proudly, interviewed at the most painful moment
Courageously assuming the burden, apologizing to your friends
For not being able to do it one last time, voice cracking, knowing, it's over…
for now.

Despite the disappointment, the slight twinkle in tearing eyes
Provides a subtle glimpse that more lessons have been learned.
The little baby that felt a soothing rubdown and heard strange words from a
new world

This proud young man, who gingerly approached each step
In his legendary journey, will move on, silently setting
His sights on the next challenge, growing each step of the way.

I will always remember the flickering frames of film in my mind,
Always embracing every precise move, each miracle finish.
But most of all, I'll remember how you dreamed,
How you worked, and how you loved.

Rumors

Tom Meschery

"He said of you," my wife says to me,
repeating the words the passenger next to her
on her flight home used, "he was the meanest
sonofabitch I'd ever seen play basketball."
Which, after we arrive home and put away
and have a bite to eat and take a nap, leaves me
examining my life for meanness: I discount
the elbows I threw in self-defense and
the occasional punch that rarely landed. I confess
some came close enough that from a distance
might have been interpreted as meanness.
Could he have witnessed me swinging a chair,
chasing the Lakers player until he ran off the court?
I'll never know what possessed me to do that,
but was it meanness? In a world in which
you never get *Do Overs*, must I be remembered
as mean? I never spanked my children hard.
I never struck my wife. My students called me
a softie, my voice rarely raising in anger.
But there was my epitaph being written
at ten thousand feet above the earth
by a stranger who might have seen me play
or maybe not at all, and just heard from someone
else that I was mean. How rumors start. How unjust
life can be, viewed through someone else's eyes.

HEROIC PLAY

Flo-Jo (Dee-Dee)

Tommy Domino

Florence Delorez (with a Z) Griffith-Joyner
Born the 7th of 11 children with a passion for painting.
Friends and family called her "Dee-Dee" raised in
The Jordan Downs Projects in Watts.

While attending the 102nd Street Elementary School
Dee-Dee would learned to skip the wind on weekends
running track with the Sugar Ray Robinson Organization.
She would later win the Jesse Owens Games back-to-back.

Her father Robert was an electrician and mother Florence
a seamstress. Dee-Dee seamlessly shocked the world with
her fierce agility and
flashy flamboyant sense of fashion. In 1987 she would marry
the Olympic high jumper
named Al Joyner and the name Flo-Jo would define an era.

Those four-inch nails that would change colors daily like
a chameleon; from fuchsia to tiger stripe to six inch red, white,
blue, and gold. Bold! The world was not ready.
But *WE* relished in it. *WE* saw ourselves in her.

One of *OURS* grew up to be the fastest woman
ever recorded with a stopwatch. 1988 was a leap year.
Doug Williams would take the big leap
as the first black quarterback to win in Super Bowl XXII.
That year the Lakers and Dodgers brought home trophies.
But Flo-Jo was the brightest star in the galaxy in 1988.
Our people's own version of Halley's Comet.

On that sunny day in Seoul September 29, 1988
She broke the world record twice in the 200-meter dash
Her feet glided on the winds of Oya.
In the end of the race, she prayed our prayers
and cried our tears.

Experts believed the breeze assisted *only* runner
#569 on that day. Causing them to add an asterisk
to her record: "Probably strongly wind assisted
but recognized as the world record."
The thirst for a witch hunt was never satiated.

I wonder, whimsical wind skipper from Watts.
I wonder if they would add an asterisk to
Babe Ruth's records though he would retire 12 years
before Jackie Robinson would break baseball's "color-line" in 1947.
Baseball had a full 71-year head start before
a black person was allowed to appear in a batter's box.

Jimmy (the Greek) Synder got canned from CBS
earlier in '88 for saying blacks were bred to be better
athletes since before the Civil War:
"The slave owner would breed his big black to his big woman
so he can have uh big black kid, see.
That's where it all started."

Black excellence cultivates a brigade of naysayers.
She went through rigorous blood analysis tests
administered by Manfred Donike, the expert on drugs and sports.
Every test came back negative. It never hushed the speculation.
All that doesn't matter.

Flo-Jo single handedly shook up the world.
Awarded the James E. Sullivan Award for top amateur athlete,
designed the Indiana Pacers' uniforms, and has two paintings at
The Art of Olympians display, 102nd Street Elementary
was renamed after her. The picture of her peaceful prayer
at the end of the race has graced every cubicle wall
I have sat at since she passed in 1998.

Angel in His Corner

Robert Eugene Rubino

Ode to Angelo Dundee, 1921–2012

Part I. London, 1963

Cassius Clay winks at Elizabeth Taylor sitting ringside
taking his eye off journeyman Henry Cooper his tough Brit foe
possessed of a wicked left hook and that wicked left hook
deposits the young buck on his American arse and the crowd crows
and although saved by the bell Cassius might've seen
his imminent shot at Sonny Liston's heavyweight title
turning into the fistic equivalent of Eddie Fisher's marriage.

But Clay has Angelo in his corner and in between rounds
his trainer buys time for his glassy-eyed rubber-legged fighter
by finding—lo and behold—a tear in one of his gladiator's gloves
and gosh who knows how long it might take to replace
well long enough for Clay's head and legs to revive
and his fists to take care of business by busting up Ol' 'Enery
in the next round thus keeping his destiny's date with Sonny.

Part II. Miami Beach, 1964

And in that title fight against the fearsome favored Bear
with Clay helplessly blinking like a man blind to his own fate
(suspicious irritant on Liston's gloves—intentionally? who knows?)
he wants Angelo to stop the fight after the fourth round
Angelo instead cleanses his fighter's eyes—won't let him quit
urges him to dance and survive and rally and transcend.
Two rounds later Clay is champ. One day later he's Ali.

Ode to the Ireland Spuds

Mike Bonifer

With love and appreciation for the Spuds
on the 60th anniversary of our memorable year

Any year that ends in '3'
carries back me to '63
when the Ireland Spuds
made their run to the Sweet 16

I will never watch the movie *Hoosiers*
without believing our version was better
Jimmy Chitwood didn't ride my school bus
Like Dave Small and Arnie Renner

Hickory didn't hang a banner
across the highway on consecutive Saturdays
where they drank beer provided by
Stan Leinenbach's uncle after their victories

Hickory's coach did not drop his pants
to make good on a crazy promise
like our Coach Pete Gill did
in front of the local populace

Hipsters in black Chuck Taylors
set contemporary fashion trends
But they'll never be as cool
as Doug Padgett or Joe Lents

Before Bill Walton UCLA'd
or Secretariat was thoroughly bred
Denny Keusch of the Ireland Spuds
set the standard for studs whose hair was red

Of men with muscular reps
dudes you're supposed to fear
I always imagine Stan and Ronny Klem
saying, Please—hold our beer

In any victory celebration
through blizzards of confetti
I can still see the smiling face
of my cousin Bill Linette

When bouncers clear a late night bar
or lawyers file a claim
I recall the firm of Eck & Voelkel
clearing out the lane

Wherever books are balanced
And the busses run on time
I give all the original credit
To Junie Wigand and Ronny Heim

A leader successful
Wherever he or she goes
Will always bring to my mind
Ireland's Principal, Mister Jim Roos

Let's hear it for these heroes
They are family
They are legend
They are blood
Anyone who was here
for that joyful year of '63
will always and forever be
an Ireland Spud

Basketball Jones
Nathanial Brian Anderson

Rickey Jones, shooting guard for Miens High School
Rickey Jones a rather prideful player
6'2' tall, 8ᵗʰ man on the team
Let him tell it

At times mellow, at times an arrogant fellow
Jones mean with dribble, cool on the defensive end
Do anything for the win when he's in the game
Do anything for the team in money green and gold
The almighty mad dogs of Miens High

Rickey Jones follows Coach P home to get on one accord
Cause he and Coach P haven't been seeing Eye to Eye
Coach P is like, Rickey, you followed me to my home
You see, Coach P usually charges a fee to see him outside school hours
Rickey explains that he's way better than Robbie
The starting shooting guard
You know Robbie P, the nephew of the coach

You know how that go
I can be better
Coach P, with the reverse of glee, says, Rickey go home
Know your place, never again talk about Robbie P

See, Rickey Jones' mouth cashes checks two weeks before payday
He keeps it up, Waterboy Jones might become the name of this poem

You feel me?

The night before the first game of the season, Rickey Jones has a dream
It is a violent storm and Rickey is lost on a b-ball court
All he can see is number 23 on a jersey
With a superhero of sorts telling him
"Play your position."
"Take your shot."

23 tells Rickey
"I was cut from my team at your stage.
And look at me. All you need is your shot.
Will you make it?"
You see, 23 is the greatest to ever to take it.

Rickey wakes up ready for the evening's game.
All day he can see 23 in his dream.
"Play your position."
"Take your shot."

Game time!
Pine time for Rickey Jones to start the game.
About a minute before the half, Coach P yells, "Rickey!"
"Play your position"
"Take your shot"
Sweat boils
Rickey steals the ball
His position
Three-point line
His shot
Buzzer sounds
It's Rickey Time

Basketball Jones…

El Leon de Culiacan

Carlos Ornelas

Growing up poor with
5 sisters and 4 brothers,
He lived in an old, abandoned railroad car.
Poverty was not enough to keep him down,
He was on his way to becoming, pound for pound,
One of the greatest warriors the world's ever seen,
Became a world champ by the age of 18.
The Caesar of Boxing, Gran Campeon Mexicano,
With a deadly left hook and titanium jaw.

Round after round,
Brawl after brawl,
One by one,
The contenders fall.

87 wins,
No draws,
No losses.
Being a champ,
Dangerous process.

His name will come-up when given the subject
Of mentioning forces no mortal should fuck with.
Among other things are hurricanes, trains,
Along with a short list of warriors' names.
Like Tyson, Ali, Marciano and such,
The club for the Men with the Deadliest Punch.
And one of those names
From the greats and the novices,
Is the Mexican Champion,
Julio Cesar Chavez.

Standing at 5-foot-7-and-a-half
68 inches away from his wrath.
An orthodox stance, a murderous glance,
Hands made from brass and obsidian glass.

The post and the ante meridiem clash,
The fists eclipse organs and glands.
The judge scores: a round each,
The crowd speaks: a foul screech,
The punches from Southeast
Can outreach a mouthpiece.

Uppercut, jab, straight,
Elbows and back straight,
Throw combinations,
Punching bag castrate.

There is no final prize,
37 title fights,
Knocked-out Neanderthals,
Cavemen and troglodytes.

But history's trends are repeated again,
And all great things must come to an end.
And all of God's men, no matter how strong,
Will witness a stronger man coming along.

Even the mightiest champion of all,
From the peak of his glory, is destined to fall.

After the lights and the champion belts,
After the pain and the bruises subside,
Standing inside of the ring by himself,
The former world champ waves a final goodbye.

Legends don't die, they just pass the baton,
Respect to El Leon de Culiacan.

Jesse Owens
Caleb Smith

an Olympian made
smoking Hitler's white race
like eighties crack cocaine
when he took first place
they said it was smoke and mirrors
his coffee color had 'em bitter
shining brighter than the white, go figure
the black folks would cry out "go nigga!"
it wasn't cocky it was competitive
had to hand those Nazis sedatives
to calm down
their Aryan supremacy shot down
ay, Adolf? who's the bomb now?
nonsense became exposed
gold medals? he's got four of those
he just had to put them on notice
Hitler's crew was made of slowness
racisms bogus, all race is equal
unless the track features
Jesse Owens

Abebe Bikila

Mike Bonifer

Abebe Bikila won the 1960 Olympic Marathon gold medal
Running barefoot through the streets of Rome
Set a new world record in bare feet
Repeated the feat in shoes
in sixty-four in Tokyo
First marathoner to go gold
Twice in a row like that

Flipped his Beetle
on an Addis Ababa highway
in sixty-nine
First a paraplegic
Then a wheelchair athlete
in table tennis and archery
Died in seventy-three
Cerebral hemorrhage, done
Age of forty-one

Abebe Bikila
Ethiopia's favorite son
Say his name in a restaurant
in Little Ethiopia
Waitress'll smile at you and
bring you extra sambu—

Wait a second—
Run it back
Return to the starting line

Abebe Bikila won
The 1960 Olympic Marathon
Barefoot!
Ran twenty-six miles, three hundred eighty five yards
Barefoot!
Forty-two point one nine five kilometers

Barefoot!
Chased by sixty men in shoes, he ran—
Barefoot!
Had shoes, they gave him blisters, so he tossed them in the trash and ran—
Barefoot!
Through the crooked cobblestoned hills of Rome
Barefoot!
Lit by torches along the Appian Way
Barefoot!
Finished at night under the Arch of Constantine
Barefoot!
In the shadow of the Coliseum
Barefoot!
Set the world record
Barefoot!
Two hours, fifteen minutes, sixteen seconds
Barefoot!
Took the gold
Barefoot!
Broke the tape and kept running on his tiptoes
Barefoot!
Said he could run another 10K, easy
Barefoot!
Ran himself into history
Barefoot!

After that—
Abebe needs a new pair of shoes
Puma walks into the room
with cash socked away in the shoes
he will wear to win in Tokyo
That is the pinnacle, the peak
In five years he'll flip the Beetle
and lose the lease on his rented feet
In four more he'll go to his glory
That's the straight-ahead story

In the story that doesn't run straight ahead
Abebe Bikila is not dead.
After breaking the tape in Rome
while still running on tiptoes
it is not in place, but into the torchlight
of a million imaginations that he runs
Is running still
In the Hills of Rome
Along Addis Ababa roads
In the restaurants of Little Ethiopia
And in this poem
Barefoot as the day he was born
Abebe Bikila

Pele

Willie June Landers

Slam the door on football locker
The real deal is called soccer
Ate a bowl of gumbo in filé
Read 'bout soul of Mr. Pele

The NFL brags on Jim Brown
While Pele really got on down
Exposed to soccer by his dad
Showed so much promise as a lad

At seventeen played in first World Cup
Bulgarians said "Beat him up
We can not stop his perfect style
We'll stop him with targeted fouls"

It worked in nineteen sixty-six
Four years later he had a fix
Despite injury, he looked up
Brazil won its rightful World Cup

Retired, nineteen seventy-four
There is, however, so much more
U. N. rep for ecology
Goodwill causes he'd often plead

He'd say "If you are first you are first"
Why in the world did he say that verse?
He follows with words that are crushing
"If you are second, you are nothing"

Hakeem Olajuwon aka Hakeem the Dream

Tom Meschery

In Africa each morning practice starts
with warm-ups. The youngest on the team,
perhaps sixteen, always the first waiting for me,
sits in the thin shade below the backboard,
reading the latest article about Hakeem.
We stretch hamstrings, then slow jog
around the court. He keeps pace, all the while
talking about The Dream. "Dis donc," he says,
"With The Dream we would defeat Senegal
and be champions of West Africa.
Que pensez vous, entraineur?" What do you think?
I can't think about anything other than the red
and smoky sun rising over the opposite basket,
the heat already sweating my shirt, and how
the rains suddenly begin halfway through practice.
I shag his jump shots, the ones he swears
are like Hakeem's. He says he too will attend
The University of Houston, later play in the NBA.
"Vous m'assistez?" But his shots are ugly, too flat;
they lack the backspin, the softness of the Dream's.
I nod my head, whatever I can do—my best shot.
I am in the country of Burkina Faso.
Its name means Land of Upright People.

Tiger Pa
Mike Bonifer

You make your pro debut
age of two
national TV
chipping balls into baskets
with a miniature club
to make Sarge proud
Merv Griffin giggle
the audience cheer loud
A high you will chase
for the rest of your days

You bring a sport for the rich
to its knees
like it's auditioning to be
your bottom bitch
Like it's been freed of a demon
at your tent revival
Win the Open by fifteen at Pebble
Win it again in oh-eight
on a broken leg
Dominate the Masters down in Georgia
where you hole an impossible chip
Pausing the ball's logo
on the lip of the cup before it drops
like it's a red carpet photo op
When a past Master makes
a watermelon joke
you send him packin'
to wherever crackers go
when they crumble
The days of Snead talking shit
about Charlie Sifford
and Lee Elder are done for

Your imagination so vivid
coaches cannot cliché
"Visualize your shot"
because you see and stroke
extravagant works of art
when a simple fade will do
You adopt a different vision
You imagine the ball coming at you
It's the solution and the problem
Isn't that true?
Like birds flock to water
balls and conquests fly your way
And who is a Cablinasian Ocean
to deny a single gull its stay?

I wonder if you foresaw
your duck-hooking SUV
from the point of view of the concrete wall
flying at you on a wounded arc
a betrayal of time and body would describe
It hasn't been the same after that, of course
Even oceans have their shores

I will always recall
a thousand heads turning in unison
uttering involuntary Whoas!
when you smoke a drive
Will remember galleries clustering
around a divot you make
with a 5-iron through
four inches of rough at Riviera
on a shot that swerves
around two trees
over a third
clears the front bunker
and stops on the green
two hundred ten yards away
like a tiptoeing burglar

finding a hidden safe
They detective that divot
like it's a clue, proof
that the crime they witnessed
is the actual truth

I hope to see you to win again
This time playing one-handed
the last five holes because
a spider bit your hand when you
fetched your ball from Thirteenth cup
This time wearing a saffron robe
after spending a year
in Tibet with Shaolin monks
who are friends of your mom's

I will settle for a periodic spark
A memory of Merv Griffin's delight
when, after grinding to make a cut
you limp home on Sunday
and hole an occasional crazy shot
A rare sighting of the electricity
that once charged the game
like potable lightning

Maybe your children
having witnessed your demise
will shine bright because of it
Their light reflecting you
The good dad
Your young cats swinging
Freely
Ferociously
Seeing the future arc their way
like a ball escaping the rough
Dodging trees and traps
to land pin high
at their feet

The Biles
Tyler Lenn Bradley

What a flip!
What a twist!
What a triple
twisting dip!
When she sat out
the Olympic
championship
and defied
America's
egotistical
chronic guilt trip
for *herself.*

Some say she quit
They don't know *shit.*

Do the Biles
take care of you
Do the Biles
Be brave
choose you.

INNERPLAY

percussion

Donny Jackson

*"What I think this comes down to is, Caster's faster than white girls
and she made them cry."*
Pidgeon Pagonis

"Suck on my balls, pause, I had enough…"
Beyoncé

bang

run   footfalls   ngoma really   then wind   a lover's lips at her
ear wind   the stadium is a shell full of ocean wind   only wind and
woman as drum   fast is music   fast music   they hear in front of
them until they can't anymore   the worst music is music you know is
playing but can't hear   so maybe she is an unholy instrument to them
and who would make room for such a thing in their sound but the tone deaf
let's puncture woman as drum with a needle   lay her skin less taut
less music we can't hear   less black as music   how do you solve a
problem like serena   yes black woman is too much ngoma   black too
fast   too drum   too we can't hear you back here   isn't it the same
song   black woman run is still a steal away to Jesus   woman music
off the plantation fast music   thought sojourner was a man too   too
much drum   fast music   it's safer if black women parade   not
run   like the 3 usa pageant winners this year   crown them to slow walk
their bodies and stand still   smile like a trophy   don't fast run music
and while we loud wind   not lover's lips not shell   about the runner
being punished   there is a man somewhere   often black too
trying to choke the boy whose parts his woman was born with until she is
dead as dick   black woman too much music in all the winds   if they
can't catch it or kill it then steal it   the runner runs anyway   she is
fast   she is a woman   she is drum   lover's lips shell to her ear
wind   so she can't even hear taylor swift and her marching band

I Love Wrestling

Kulani Dudley

I love wrestling because I love math
and science
I love long equations and using formulas to
solve them
I love the guarantee of an answer
right or wrong, one will be there
I love wrestling because I love puzzles
and word problems and riddles
I love dissecting something to put it back together
over and over and over again
until it's damn near perfection
I love staring at what I've completed in pride
with a grin on my face
satisfied with what I've accomplished

I love wrestling because as a child I played
with fire, I pinched my fingers together
to put out a burning candle wick
held the palm of my hand over a flame until it shrunk
stared at the swaying smoke of incense
until it went out, and held hot cups of tea until my hands burned
I love wrestling because a heat inside
of my chest grows, my skin becomes fire-y
steam fills the air
and a flame of passion gets wilder and wilder
in the forest-fire that spreads to my hands and my feet

I love wrestling because I love water
I've spent hours and hours on end
in the ocean, in pools, in lakes
The happy place I go to in my head is
under water, diving or swimming in the depths
picking up rocks from a sanded ocean-ground
and seeing how long I can hold my breath while hovering above a pool floor

I love wrestling because nothing
makes me love water more than wrestling
cool brisk water quenching my tired dry throat
after a day of hard hard work

Everything that I have loved lies in wrestling.

Chess Mind
Jeff Rogers

Chess Mind Knows

How imagination's strong fingers press, probe,
Massage tense future, knead loose blockages,
Free up tingly range and flow of possibility.

Chess Mind Knows Too

How the board can be checkered with overlaid shadows
Of the possible; how these shadows can blur and blind you
Or bustle you jostle you forward toward a layered sight.

Ready, Aim...
Sutichai Savathasuk

The wind whistles.
Feet planted firm onto ground,
rooted to connect
a straight line
from your soles to top of head.
Shoulders relaxed,
gut tucked in,
prepared
to bow.

Ready.

Standing straight in a row,
nock on string. Arms raised,
steady,
perpendicular to the lines
drawn on your back
like constellations
guiding you truly.

Aim.

Your thumb caresses your cheeks,
locked beneath your chin,
pulling the tension,
creating potential energy
to launch your shaft flocking feathers.
Transferring the hold / your breath in
sights guided by the eye
of the storm, a windy path between
your shot to point blank,
Silence.

Fire.

J.U.M.P.
Julia Mallory

They taught me how to fly
between the ropes
slope my shoulder
between the bubble
of telephone cord
two bookends sturdy
their hands turning
conjuring rhythm
flipping frequencies
to the center
of the pavement
I'm in a portal baby
kicking up the ashes
of my adversaries
jumping hard
levitating
no hesitation
betcha can't do it like thiiiiiiis
bouncing in the air
three-sixty pivot
on the balls of my feet
call and repeat
kinesthetic cosmology
our melanated bodies glowing
in the summer sun

evening run
Brynna Boyd

In case the street lights flickered on
I dressed up to be seen,
A view for those who passed along,
A scream of "Look at me!"

That echoed—no one to hear it,
And wound through empty parks.
I was a painting in an attic,
A mural in the dark.

I was off display, though under
light, my shadow is not neared
My efforts go unfulfilled.
I am the only viewer.

When I met myself along that trail,
It struck me with surprise
I seemed less a spectacle,
More a phantom unconfined.

Ballin'

Anthony Crespo

It used to be why I would wake up in the morning
Why I would be excited to go to school
Damn…I remember it being
the only reason I would go to school
I used to pour water into Tupperware
Mix in dishwashing soap
and use my extra toothbrush to scrub the dirt
off my basketball shoes until they looked brand-new
I used to set out my clothes the night before
One pair for looking
fresh in the hallways
and one for sports.
I remember wearing my jeans over my
basketball shorts and double-layering my shirts
so I could take off my cool clothes fast
and be ready to ball
Outdoor school yards in the morning
Indoor courts at lunch time
Rec centers in the afternoon
Lacing up all day!
From neighborhood streetball to YMCAs
From double rims with chains that ring
like cash registers when you score
to netless hoops that offer no praise
like rain on sunny days.
From uneven half courts
to polished wooden floors
where the legendary SWOOOOOSH applauds
as leather skin brushes against diamond-patterned polyester
That short, sweet sound of victory

Playing close to home was always the safer bet
but we enjoyed the danger and drama
of walking onto the painted concrete
that other kids defended with elbows and shoving
travels and double-dribbles

The occasional fight was always a part of the fun
Choosing a friend you knew had your back was important
When that playful rectangle turns into a squared circle
you need someone you can go to war with
Someone you don't have to tell where to pass
To set a pick
To swing when you're at the top of the key
To rush the board when you're shooting a three
Or when you break someone's ankles
and take it to the hole
That feeling!
of floating above the ground when I sway, shake
and dance through my opponents
sketching an improvised masterpiece with my feet
The touch of the ball as I sew it through my legs
and around my back
The ferocity of my mentality when I begin my attack
To the right
to the left
to the right again
fake left
then spin
boost of acceleration!
I drive
I slice through wind
I fly
I walk on air
I'm high!!!
Then release
like I'm setting the ball free
Letting go of control
Praying it finds its way home
Like me
When I'm ballin'

Basketball was my family when I needed family the most
The friends I laughed and played with
when I didn't want to feel alone
taught me the lessons only the game can teach

Will always remind me that life is fun
I still ball
Not like I used to
But I can always count on basketball
to make me feel alive and young
Let's ball!

The Shot

Davion Moore

Coming up the court
Eyes darting
Palms sweating
Mind moving
A mile a minute
Time is ticking
But seconds
Feel like an eternity
An array of emotions
Cloud my thinking
Yet I have to stay focused
On the task at hand
I pass the ball
To my teammate
Who quickly dribbles
And looks around
Stalling
As I break free
From my defender
They pass the ball to me
As I move toward
The basket
I have the shot
We wanted
But I feel a little scared
Because all eyes are on me

This is too much pressure
And I am unsure
That I can handle it
What if I miss the shot?
And cost my team the game
And the state championship?
What if I fail?
I can't do this

I should pass it
And let someone else take the shot
But my team is depending on me
To take the shot
I think of the greats
And what they would do
Air Jordan would take the shot
The Black Mamba would take the shot
Chef Curry would take the shot
Regardless
If it goes in or not
So what do I have to do?
Take the shot
I take a mid-range jumper
Letting it fly
Whatever happens
Happens
The clock winds down
3!
2!
I focus on the ball
As it sails to the hoop
1!
And feel like my eyes deceive me
As it goes in the hoop
The crowd erupts
I am like a statue
In awe of what just happened
My teammates rush towards me
I'm still in shock
I really did it
We really did it
We won!
My teammates hug me
My coach pats me on the back
I look in the stands
My parents are going crazy
We got the win

All it took
Was for me to believe in myself
Fear and doubt will come along
But if you trust in yourself
You can achieve
The impossible
Believe me
I know

Surrenderance

Takayla P. Carlton

"Girl you gon catch a cold out there in that rain!"
I can hear momma's voice echoin in my mind
as if I was still all legs and lip
what she describes as my eleven-year ol' self
Can hear her sayin I must've lost my mind
That I done got my hair all wet n she
not heatin tha hot comb up again

But ion care none

I ran in tha rain today
Felt freedom for tha first time
Strides long like tha Nile itself
Chest out
        Chin high
                Clouds gatherin

                                God roarin

Blessin each splash peckin at my ankles
Glasses opaque n speckled wit drops
When I could no longer see
n my limbs began to pout from exhaustion
I found it easier to just   surrender
To let spirit n wind guide my steps rather than runnin against it

I felt safe in tha middle of tha storm

I felt free

Why I'm Not a Baseball Star

Jeff Rogers

"How could you tell who was going to make it?" someone asks the youth baseball coach.

"If they wanted to be in the batting cage more than with a naked woman," he says.

"Now I know why I never made it," I say.

DANGEROUS GAMES

Thomas Hearns' Right Hand

Romus Simpson

wide in the face
flat and heavy
freight falling fifteen feet onto the docks
a plough hitting a stone in a dark field
jerking the tractor round
blind and cattycornered
as two Cadillacs met
coiled in a wide intersection
V-8's still revving
pimps all a scatter
featherclad and undone

it sent anyone spinning who got it
caught that flash of weight
and bore it reshaped
collapsed in the rising numbness
the bright end of war moving across
the variable interim like luminous lungs
jettisoned earth sphere in an atomic dreamscape
scattered and expanding
the new strange body blue
eyeless and crying

it was profanity among women
flowering exponentially inappropriate and red
the shrieking inhale of men
suddenly at blows with each other
it was like yanking the house left
the table scooting then toppling
hurrying fruit
the salt shakers tilting losing it
a rotating chair swinging hard west
into a large mirror
…and the mirror going crazy

Suckerpunched

Pam Ward

It never fails.
Every time you think
you'll just lounge
you'll just stay
and lie down for the count
and just bask in that
sure felt good glow.
No, that's when they
leap up, zip pants
lace their Nikes
click the ball game on
or CNN news
and hand you your bus pass or shoes.
But it never fails, girlfriend
when you pull a Mike Tyson on them
when you do the whore move
roll over and get your car keys
before they come good
walk with sure-footed strut
of a ring girl
and say "bye" without batting a lash
they act like they've been jabbed
had their face splashed with water
They act like you kicked out their wind
looking stunned
clutching blankets
all close to their chin
saying, "You're leavin'?
You're just going to jump in your clothes?
You're just going to fuck me and leave?"
And them left hooks start flyin'.
And they hit you with lines like
"But baby, my sugar sweet pumpkin pie love
please don't go." Lip to ear
he starts whispering, "baby…
we're sure make some pretty fine kids."

You'll switch roles.
He'll switch channels
find a good flick that's on
ask if you've had something to eat.
So jump back
jab 'em quick
if you want to stay long
Act as bold as the wild
steely locks of Don King
cuz the one on their feet
calls the shots.

Murder Ball

Carlos Ornelas

Here's a game only the ghetto can make,
If you ever heard its name, it's not a mistake.

Step right up, street children,
Come one and come all.
I'll teach you to play the game, murder ball.

Yes, you heard right, all you need is a ball,
The green ones for tennis will work best of all.
You need a wall and a a few of your friends,
Peep how street kids start the scariest trends.

All you got to do to play is throw the damn ball,
And then try to catch it when it bounces off the wall.

But if you try to catch the ball and it falls to the ground,
Everyone has the right to start beating you down.

They will only stop beating you when your hands touch the wall,
This will repeat each time it may fall.

You will get penalized the third time that you drop it,
You must stand against the wall with your hands in your pocket.

This is the part of the game that gets odd,
Your opponents become like a firing squad.

They each take a turn, standing in line,
Throwing the ball at you, one at a time.

Here is a game where everyone loses,
Walking away in pain and with bruises.

All you need is a wall and a green tennis ball,
Just don't let it fall,
This is…murder ball.

The Female Boxer

Caleb Smith

they tried to put her in this box
she told them, "put me in the ring"
sports bra and all, call her Leila Ali
she float like a butterfly,
sting like queen bee
quick feet, but she don't flee
gettin hers amongst the hes
they ask if the hits are fine,
saying she's fragile
she said,
"i dodge em
when they hit my line.
child, i'm agile."
she was never one to tap out
when they clap back
she dumped the tap shoes,
but girl could still dance
as the so-called underdog
and puncher's chance
she makes love with her gloves,
how's that for romance?
the men mock, the women rant
she simply talks with her hands
action verbs ya heard
their words don't grant her permission

she says "what she's capable of
is God's decision"
a man's world, doesn't rock hers
a K.O. never knocked her
they always tryna put her in this box
funny now
         she's a boxer

Nightmare on Queen St.
Dante Mitchell

Wake up in the jungle
Clouds of marijuana
Knight in damaged armor
Fighting with anacondas
I could keep a soul full of pride on the Metro rail
Expect no fails
My will to achieve my goals
I must excel
Roughest tales from the memories of bucket pales
Full of sand at Queens Park
Rusted nails & bolts held the goal together
The floor was dressed with
ashes, blood, and sweat
Bloods in sets
Derek D left open was wet (swish)
Rob Johnson was the most athletic
Bingo with the dime to Mark elbow connection
Davion & Marquis were 'Hot Sauce' and 'Bone Collector'
Nicholas controlled the pace
made sure the tempo was set
DeVonte was a corner threat
Jeremy shooting threes like Hornaceck
I was always the last picked up
too young to pose a threat
But I played on the court when Joseph pledged to red
Loss of a childhood friend still haunts my head
Grew older realized the morbid hex amongst the people
I've seen men's souls go void when consumed by evil

The Pugilist

Anthony Crespo

I wear stories on my face
Legends written with broken bone soaked in the blood of battle
Like petroglyphs carved into the hardened rock of my body
Etched in the scars on my knuckles
Chiseled into the restless clenching of my fists
Heard in the cracks when I close them
Bend my wrists
my neck
my back
knees and ankles my movements are loud
like percussion
But smooth like light midnight jazz
My feet dance to the rhythms of the space around me
Pay. Attention.
Hear the pain and savagery in my foot steps
Splintered joints beating each other like djembes marching to war
Feel the sharp slice of my gaze
See the brutal bite of my jaw
tallness of my prideful posture
wideness of my broadened shoulders
I wear like armor I dress myself in every morning
in case today is the glorious day
when I'm carried away on my
shield.

The fables of a fighter are hidden in the fractures of my skull
The crooked ridges of my orbitals, cheek bones, brows and septum
Glimpsed in the dark reflections of eyes
surrounded by pinched lines that come to life
when I focus
or stare.
Read the Sanskrit carved in the small cuts
around the edges of my
lips
Words spoken in a language that no dialect could ever describe

No dialect ever could describe the heart of a warrior.
The fears he conquers
when death is delivered in every blow
Every shot that shocks his senses
Every attack on his defenses
There are no synonyms for the primal adrenaline
surging through the veins of gladiators
fighting to be free
Boxers boxing their way out of the boxes
civilization tries to put us
in
The only way to win
is to face an enemy that looks like me
Bleeds like me
for a bloodthirsty crowd roaring as their inner lions awaken
Applauding and chanting for the violence
they only wish they could
be a part of
Only champions enter that ring of fire
brave enough to walk through
the flames of victory
only obtained by the few
who walk out
with their souls still attached.

Car Fight 59

Pam Ward

I like L.A., particularly
the car racing in residential areas.
The last one was with this obnoxious slob
in a white gloss Benz.
Cut me off big time.
Him and his fat cigar
and Barbie bitch
glued to his lap.
Passed me with one hand.
I had to brake so hard
my groceries wrecked
in the backseat.
It really pissed me off
but I got back next to em
and blasted the most
ghetto rap tape I had.
Slide all the windows down
started bobbing too
like I gave a fuck
acting oblivious
to his dog-faced mug
and his stuck-up date.
I waited in the right lane
foot hovering the gas
like a crook
ready to smash it down
the second that sucker went green.
Wasn't even where I wanted to go.
But sometimes you gotta show folks
let em know
we all own these streets
even if it means
taking in extra scenery.

BEAUTIFUL PLAY

Volleyball Season 2013/23

Brynna Boyd

with my hands,   I make gentle work of

jammed thumbs, strong fingers   the game, a warm companion,

my team, a watchful eye   waits for me—

I owed them   myself in whole

my body's limits   finding joyful space for

sweat-soaked shirts and   fourteen kids ready with

feet quick enough to   *Go! Yay! Jump! Slay!*

make smooth hops passed   memories

the vomit on the bleachers—   replaced with laughter

my daily prayer   a game turned a game

to *look* the part   of coach

on the court, a stage   and players, simply playing

my heroine's objective   a first love for sport

slim   then a growing, beating, heart

toned, and never   quitting, or only finding rest

foul-tongued   for moments, between the glee,

a story made tragic   relative to perfection

she descends slowly   they are still wanderers

in the crowd   practicing a communal project

fatigued, misguided but   never

Alone

La Belle

Dan Yu

In fencing, "La Belle" means the deciding point.
Fencing bouts go to either 5 or 15.
At 4-4 or 14-14, there is only one more touch.
Fencers are usually spent.
This is about the moment right before
the referee says, "Allez!" or "Fence!"

sweat drips down my face
we've pushed and pulled
for what seems like forever
though I know it's been only minutes.

28 touches have been scored
many more chances missed
some were late, some were mistakes
both good and bad.

I ache, wanting this to be over
my feet are on fire
my opponent also has
their hands on their knees.

"La ligne, s'il vous plait!"
the referee implores
I straighten and slowly
walk to the en garde line.
"En garde!"
the mask goes down

"Pret?"

It's 14-14.

Breathe.

Bobby

Tom Meschery

For Randall

It's worth mentioning that he was small for his age
and scurried around the basketball court
like a mouse, a pet if we had held him in our hands
and gave him comfort. But we often ridiculed him
for the little gestures that he made with his fingers
on either side of his mouth where where whiskers
would appear in our thoughtless imaginations.
It is worth mentioning that he carried letters
and stood behind the counter of his post office
and sent our important missives to their important
destinations, all the while keeping faith
with those years on the basketball court
Most of us grew fat, our legs turning to mush,
so that we could hardly run, in my case, walk.
Bobby won championships shooting hoops,
Sixties and Over; *Seventies and Over*;
Three on Three; *Free Throw Shooting*;
H.O.R.S.E.; bringing home medals and trophies.
It's worth mentioning that Bobby never forgot
a single moment on the court or any player
that was worthy of his admiration. His memory
brought him joy and those accomplishments
whether so slight in our youth, in his old age,
grew larger into a garden of delight.
Is it worth mentioning that few men his age
(What is he now? Eighty?) can sight over the ball
measure the distance to the hoop and score
as if the distance between his eye and the rim,
however difficult, were the measure of the man.
Is it worth mentioning that we are not so far removed
from our youthful venality that we can not
be forgiven, which Bobby has done with every
shot he swished the net because it was the sport
we played together, and he guarded us so tightly.

on sunrise

Brynna Boyd

I'd never written poems about sunrise
I was never awake for it,
and I had a definite bias to sunsets—
to the end of the day, to closing chapters
to whatever allure or wonder or mystery lurked in the night
or under my bed or behind my pillow
but I never wrote about sunrise until that summer
when morning dew took its place in my mind
when I gained a newfound appreciation for bird chirps and wind chimes
and cool air that finds me despite my tired eyes

In flashes, I found myself writing about sunrise
watching my shadow shrink rather than my reflection fade
thinking about new beginnings over ending days
a world that we can co-create
with leaf eaters, pencil breakers, and whatever other way there is to say
that their thoughts begin in the places my mind goes faint
that they know how to write about freedom, when I only know restraint
and I knew this from the start, yet it still met me with surprise
to see the future do somersaults or seep through my blinds
and the next time I write about what awaits me
maybe it will be as natural as sunrise
as pleasant as sunrise

I'll replace mourning ends with morning lights
I'll borrow the sparkle in your eye
for a moment
and you can wear my shades
and we'll run through the sunrise
jump through sunrise
skip, talk, draw, and play through sunrise

and we'll leave the sunset poems to Dickinson
to Eliot, Poe, and Whitman
let them stay in old English and old times

and let new days begin
with Sunrise
authored by a dozen kids
written in their own language

untouched by darkness.

KD

Tom Meschery

From our seats
beneath the basket
watching KD
before the game,
I'm wondering
where I have seen
such fluid grace before,
almost like liquid,
as if Durant
was out to prove
the truth
inscribed on Keats' tombstone:
*Here lies one whose name
is writ in water.*

The Heaven of Runners
Caroline Wellman

For Dan and Dean

Dreaming again of life in the body,
they gather here as if for the first time:
records forgotten, glory forsaken.
They listen again to their own footfalls
and breath, to the heart's steady percussion,
every impulse attuned to their motion,
so absorbed that animals know them
as part of the landscape, accustomed
to their presence, as to a passing train
or wind tangled in the pines. Before them,
the world turns dreamlike: trees deepen
to autumn hues, woodpeckers thrum away
in the distance, leaves trickle down in slow
perfect spirals. They glide on soft grass,
they laugh to find themselves free of all limits.
They catch their next wind, they surge again.

The God of His Game
Frank Allocco

He was born on a concrete schoolyard
Weaned at a tender age and thrust into the athletic jungle.
Mostly watching, imitating his older heroes,
Biding his time until his moment arrived.
I watched his meteoric ascent to the pinnacle of every level he entered.
They marveled at his finely sculptured frame
And shouted at his every creative move
Toward the ever present ten foot objective.
The leather ball seemed to be an appendage to his oversized hands
As he dribbled and passed to a free education, fame, and fortune.
Like a fine wine, he improved with age.
We saw him as indestructible then as
We read of his new life of riches and bright lights.
The asphalt jungle he struggled to leave behind remained
Now filled with budding athletes once like him
All possessing the same dream he had thousands of games ago.
But time moved on, the bounces became inconsistent,
The Nureyev leaps were too few and far between.
Mortality zeroed in with a vicious vengeance and
He refused to honor the signs.
Nightly he dressed, praying for that magical moment
When, like an orchestra, the body and mind join as one
To transcend the physical limits.
Despite his impassioned pleas, it never happened…
The cheers turned to jeers as
He continually defended his prolonged decline.
He finally faded into oblivion, clutching his memories and
Tales of the rise and fall of his personal dynasty.
He returned to the playgrounds and hours of games and
Many forgot, but I remember, and delight in the trips through time
When I saw him glide through space
Defying laws of motion and controlling his destiny…
The god of his game, if he only knew
Of the joy he gave and the respect he earned
From those of us who always knew.

Jay-sus
da boogie man

when there's no way to get to the hole
when there's two seconds left on the clock
when the only way to win is a three
there's only one person you can trust
he's the patron saint of the perimeter
known on courts all over the world as
jay-sus
the arc of his shot is so exact he once hit a jay
over a dude eight feet tall from behind the three point line
while lying on his back and signing an extension to his contract
if the ball touches the rim when it goes in he apologizes for the miss
he snaps nets so frequently he was allowed to patent the sound
SWISSSSSHHH
whether off a pick-in-roll or with a hand in his face
he has impeccable aim
basketball passed a rule to make him pass the ball
so rebounding would still be a part of the game
defenders tremble at the sound of his name
jay-sus
he turns zones into a valley of dry bones
teams even cover him when he's on the bench
because he once buried a three while sitting at home
off the ball he's forever moving from one pick to another
a quick cutback and his hand is the air waiting to be discovered
out of the corner of an eye his teammate spies
his fingertips waving spiritually
his posture is poetic and personifies the words "believe in me"
the opponent's coach is screaming, "who let him get free?"
while the fat lady sings Que Sera Sera, what will be will be

Galactic Moves

Wynter Eddins

Only way is
forward.
Only way is
through.
This is
nothing new.

Backwards
is not an option.
No one can opt in
better than you.
Stand
and get through.

You can.
Only way is
to demand better.

Never give in.
Begin. Start.
Give all your heart.
Have a voice.
Use it.
Don't
abuse it.

Be
true to you.
Discover
something new.
Inside
it calls. Answer.

Love
never
stalls.

Swish

Troy R. Legette

The highlight is the power of finishing
Engaged in a fast break 3-on-2
Or 2-on-1.

Complete control in each dribble:
Right to left, left to right…
Driving to the basket.

Options flashing quicker than every step.
Questions bubbling from the adrenaline rush.

There is a difference between skills and talent:
Skills are what practice develops over time.
Talent is the natural-born coordination of skills.

The game is the happiness and competitiveness of the challenge.
Each minute adds to the set time for 4 quarters.

Strategy defines the playbook.
Experience builds the confidence for the greatest performance.

Some coaches say defense is the best offense.
Some coaches expect education to be the priority.

On the court, man-to-man stimulates high intensity.
A zone protects against deliberate penetration.

Good sportsmanship reflects great character:
Accepting the win or loss after giving all within.

Great leadership begins with great students.
Students who listen follow directions and trust the process.

Every captain was that student at some point.
Personal growth evolves into a unified body—the team.

The collective collaborates in unison.
Regulated in an organized manner, playing under the whistle.

Laying up the ball against the backboard with right or left,
Spreading the fingers on the ball for a jump shot
Through the net. Swish!

when i am shooting like this

Romus Simpson

what do i have?
my jumper
under these lights
in starlit parks
on crystal frigid nights
like gospel in conception
i fling a galaxy by my might
moonswirl when i hit
oh, how tight the function of my wrist
sensual az light rain
a testament to my beauty
when i am shooting like this

& what a legend i will make
when the game iz through
what gothic stories reverberate
of men who went for 36
of men who
despite all hostile bodies
& reaching hands
rose & sank the 2
& each jumper iz new
iz gold in the pointguard's mouth
an eazy walk
an illicit kiss
what grand elegance
what shimmering history
when i am shooting like this

all iz all
release, oh, release the shot
oh, how the rim iz hunted amidst the
velvet swirl of the spinning ball
& time
step behind me

for tonight i cannot miss
in this small corner of the vacant city
i own all physics & aim
when i am shooting like this

Flight

F. Douglas Brown

Basketball, like memory,
>> Will sometimes take
>>>> Your breath, spin it

So small it becomes the gum
>> You smack when Ronnie dances
>>>> Mid-air, orange gem cuffed

Between his wristband and right
>> Bicep. Memory, like hoops, dribbles
>>>> Back to the hours before:

You, just a kid swinging
>> From the branch of Ronnie's
>>>> Outstretched goodness.

And later, when his wide smile dunks
>> On a fool, it is easy to love the game
>>>> Memory casts. So easy to love a man

Who can jump to the gym
>> Lights, and find God watching
>>>> From the rafters. Easy to call him

Your brother's best friend
>> Mid-glide, mid-wild and crowded
>>>> Applause. Your brother shares

The court with Ronnie, and his joy holds
>> His homie's winning hammer, hardwood
>>>> Trophy of youth high above

The flashback. Is this why
>> You've come back? Does recollection
>>>> Take Ronnie's flight, or his fight

With cancer? Years and years after
        A hot gym's roar & glow is gone,
                Your brother tells you Ronnie's life

Is done, and he folds
        His hands so still, he might
                As well be done, too. Where are your

Brother's pumping fists, his hi-fives
        Always finding Ronnie's
                Palms long past a tourney,

Hoops or golf?
        Where is your Brother's adoration for a light
                Skinned black boy, laced in

Ewings, rising above a sweaty nest
        Of spikes and barbs? Basketball,
                With all its heartbreak, gasps,

Turnovers, is still like memory:—
        A selected tally. And how lucky
                To witness both game-winning

Events—your brother loving this
        Brother until life's buzzer sounds.
                You, the spectator to brotherhood changing

Points. Brotherhood breaking toward
        A beautiful conjured moment that two
                Men carry and throw down a cylinder.

My body is...
Gia Civerolo

My body
My body is
My body is young
My body cartwheels across
the park's green grass
A World War One rusted green cannon
is where I stand like a winner's podium
waving at cars, hoping they notice me

My body
My body is
My body is swimming in pools
on my back to blue ribbons
My body still slices through
borrowed pools. 100 laps
Clouds stop to watch me

My body
My body is
My body is strong, flowing and diving
through ocean waves
Racing dolphins who stop to perform just for me
They fly through the water, away
no matter how much I plead

My body
My body is
My body is able to create life
Labor is worse than running a marathon
The prize smiles
Making your heart race, sing, and cry

My body
My body is
My body is getting old but still knows what to do

How to dance and move
Stretching across the past
Reaching on tippy-toes to the future

My body
My body is
My body is strong
My body is not wrong
My body is all I want it to be
despite what the magazine covers
might say to me

My body
My body is
My body is beautiful
My body is beautiful
My body is beautiful

About the Poets

Aiyana Sha'niel is a modern spoken word artist born and raised in Los Angeles, California. She released her first body of work, *Little Black Poetry Book*, before the age of 20.

A former football player at UCLA, **AKoldpiece** vanquishes crime while spitting poetry as his family sleeps safe at night.

A Taino Puerto Rican American poet living in Long Beach, California, **Anthony Crespo** is an athlete and a creative, who builds unity in our communities, and encourages people to believe in their dreams.

Brynna Boyd is a teacher who loves helping students find their voices and explore their creative power. Her writing is informed by her everyday lived experiences and musings of better worlds.

Caleb Smith is a Houston-grown, Austin-based, physical education teacher and spoken word artist. For more of his work, you can find him @theblacksmithpoetry on all socials.

The founder and owner of Mama's Kitchen Press, the publisher of this anthology, **Camari Carter Hawkins** is a poet and writer from South Central, Los Angeles. She is the author of *Death by Comb* and the guided journal, *Write Back to You.* Her works have appeared in *Rise: An Anthology of Power and Unity, The Best of The Poetry Salon 2013-2018, Obsidian,* and elsewhere.

Carlos Ornelas is a Mesoamerican artist and author from Lynwood, California. His poetry is a vivid representation of the smiles and cries experienced growing up in Los Angeles as an underprivileged youth.

CarltonTheMessenger is a poet who showcases his unique blend of comedic poetry and storytelling into a form he calls Stand Up Poetry.

A Special Education teacher in Los Angeles, **Carole Leila Cramer** is a proud mom of four adult children and two grandchildren (River Alora Banks & Dakota Castillo Banks). She has written five books, including two books of poetry, *The Ebb & Flow of Life: Stages of Walking in Your Power* and *Insanity & Butterflies.*

Caroline Wellman's poetry collection *Presences* was published by Parallel Press in 2014, and her most recent poems have appeared in *Anthology Magazine, Big Wing Review, The Hopper, Peatsmoke Journal,* and *Seashores International* haiku journal.

Cory Cofer is a poet and storyteller who blends his distinct voice and deep rooted origins into his sought-after writings and performances. His debut collection of poetry—*Dreaming Under Polka-Dot Stars*—was published in January 2023 by World Stage Press.

Cynthia Alessandra Briano is Founder of Love On Demand Global and Director of Rapp Saloon Reading Series First Fridays. She teaches at California State University Fullerton in the Ethnic Studies Program as lecturer in the African American Studies Department.

da boogie man, a National Poetry Slam Individual Champion, retired undefeated on *It's Showtime at the Apollo,* recorded a duet with Lionel Richie, and is author, educator, playwright and therapist. His most current works are a play and book of poetry entitled *Dear James,* inspired by quotes from James Baldwin.

After 44 years as a competitor and 37 as a coach, **Dan Yu** retired from fencing. He admits to still dreaming "in fencing," but during waking hours, is fully distracted by pickleball.

Dante Mitchell is a teacher, public speaker, writer, performance and recording artist, Prince of the Ghetto, who writes his own music and edits his videos. He is most proud of giving back to his community.

As a retired veteran of both the Navy and Army, **Darryl Lewis** has found solace in poetry and performance for mental well-being, driving his lifelong passion for self-expression through poetry and singing.—*Phil 4:13*

Davion Moore is an Ohio native who recently finished his Master's degree in Sports Journalism. When he is not reading or writing, he is most likely watching a basketball game.

Donny Jackson is a poet, psychologist, and Emmy Award-winning television producer based in Los Angeles.

Eric DeVaughnn is a father, author, educator, and poet. All his poems are cracked teeth, dusky yellow and receding gum line lying limp on waxy, bright white paper, speckled red.

A former college poet with a background in improv comedy, **Evan Gore** used his creative writing talent to become a little-known TV animation writer, and an even less-known TV documentary producer. His poem, *Losing Cousins* in this anthology is his first to be published.

An advisor for the Lorca Latinx Poetry Prize and the boards for Beyond Baroque and Cultural Daily, **F. Douglas Brown** is the author of two poetry collections. His book, *Zero to Three*, was selected for the 2013 Cave Canem Poetry Prize. He teaches at Loyola High School of Los Angeles, where he serves as the Director of the Office of Equity and Inclusion.

An All-State athlete in three sports at New Providence (NJ) High School, a quarterback on Notre Dame's 1973 National Championship Football team and a guard on the Fighting Irish's basketball team, **Frank Allocco** was recognized as National High School Coach of the Year during his 24-year high school coaching career. Today he is the Executive Senior Associate Athletic Director at the University of San Francisco.

Gia Civerolo is a Los Angeles based poet, producer, educator, mother and special needs advocate. She is proud to have self-published her first full-length collection of poetry, *She Confuses Lovers, Movies, Angels & Poems*, available on Amazon. She can be seen performing at open mics around Los Angeles.

James Coats is a poet, performer, and educator born in Los Angeles and raised in California's Inland Empire. With a passion for all things creative, he strives to capture authentic self-expression through his imagistic narrative poetry.

Jeff Rogers used to walk a mile across the snowy Michigan State campus to see Magic Johnson play at musty old Jenison Fieldhouse on cold nights when his stepdad handed off the season tickets, before moving to LA in 1983 where he followed the Showtime Lakers. He's the author of *Right Wrong Night Song,* published by World Stage Press.

Julia Mallory (she/they) is a storyteller working with a range of media from text to textiles. She is the founder of the creative container, Black Mermaids, and serves as the Senior Poetry Editor for *Raising Mothers* and a Poetry Editor for *The Loveliest Review.*

Kulani Dudley was a high school wrestler in Buena Park, California.

As a data scientist and poet, **LaCole Foots** likes to let her curiosity drive her pursuits. She recently founded a data analytics start-up for social good and published her first book, *Heavy Light.*

Lester Graves Lennon is the poetry editor for *Rosebud Magazine* and an investment banker. He is a member of the board of directors of the Community of Writers. His third poetry book, *Lynchings: Postcards From America,* was published in 2022.

Marilyn "Quinoaa" Wilson Hamasu is a poet/ spoken word artist, certified integrative nutrition health coach, and watercolor artist living in Los Angeles. Her first poetry book collection will be published through the Community Literature Initiative in 2025.

Mark Gozonsky is a writer living in Mar Vista, California, who contributes freelance features to *The Los Angeles Times.* His work has also appeared in *The Sun, The Santa Monica Review,* and *Best American Sports Writing 2020.* He is the author of *The Gift is to the Giver: Reflections on a 21ˢᵗ Century Decade.*

Marlana-Patrice Pugh Hamer, a native Clevelander now residing
in Phoenix, is a poet, writer, author, performer, and educator who loves
sharing her talents with diverse audiences. Her debut poetry book is *Taking
Off My Black & White Saddle Shoes: Cleveland Poems.*

Michael Kim Roos is Professor Emeritus of English at The University
of Cincinnati Blue Ash College. He is a songwriter, poet, scholar, and
author of two books—*One Small Town, One Crazy Coach* and *Reading
Hemingway's A Farewell to Arms.*

The editor of this anthology, **Mike Bonifer,** is a poet and storyteller based
in Los Angeles whose work cooks his heartland roots in the seasonings he
has acquired traveling and experiencing the world. His first collection of
poetry, *White Men My Age,* will be published by World Stage Press in 2025.

Mike Sonksen is a poet, professor, journalist, historian and tour guide
who teaches at Woodbury University, where he serves as the Coordinator
of the school's First Year Experience Program.

Molimau Andrew Fatu aka "Usolosopherr," is a poet and alumnus of
the Community Literature Initiative whose latest book, *Underground Samoan
Orator,* will be released soon.

A sharp salesman by day, at night **Nathanial Brian Anderson**
becomes a Maverick of the Microphone in open mic poetic passion and
rhythmic rhyme with the prowess of a MC. Pay in-depth attention and be
entertained.

Pam Concepcion grew up playing softball in Metro Manila, Philippines,
for 13 years. Her poem *Field of Dreams* was awarded Best Literary Piece in
Poetry for her university's 2020–2021 academic year.

Pot stirrer, disruptor, artist/activist **Pam Ward** avoided hard time by
focusing on writing instead. She is a UCLA grad, California Arts Fellow
and Pushcart Poetry nominee. Her poetry book, *Between Good Men & No
Man At All,* is just the tip of the iceberg. www.pamwardwriter.com.

Philosophy (@philosophystyle) is an accomplished and debonair poet whose many credits include TV One's *Verses & Flow;* opening act for Grammy winner Gary Clark Jr. and songstress Alice Smith; and opening act for world-renowned poet, Saul Williams, on his *Martyr Loser* tour.

Ravina Wadhwani is a proud first-generation South Asian American author and mental health therapist residing in Long Beach, California, with roots in the U.S. Virgin Islands. She is the recipient of the Long Beach Best Poetry Collection Prize for her book, *Yellow.*

Robert Eugene Rubino is a retired newspaper copy editor and sports columnist and the author of three poetry collections, including *Douglas Knocks Out Tyson.* He's smart enough to solve The New York Times crossword puzzle on Mondays (other days, not so much).

Among his many credits, **Romus Simpson** has been published in *Callaloo, Stanford University's Black Arts Quarterly, Air/Light Magazine, University of Southern California Anthology,* and the *Voices From Leimert Park* anthology. He is the recipient of the Sara Henderson Hay Literary Prize, the Ann Stanford Poetry Prize, The Nancy Hayes Poetry Prize, and the Palabra Poetry Prize.

Ron L. Dowell holds two Master's degrees from California State University Long Beach. In 2017, he received the UCLA Certificate in Fiction Writing, and in 2022, World Stage Press published his poetry collection, *Watts UpRise.* Ron is a 2018 PEN America Emerging Voices Fellow.

Saint Ice began his writing and performing journey at the age of 19 as founding member of the 1980's pioneering hip-hop ensemble The Rapper's Rapp Group. The dapper Los Angeles native shares his emotionally-intelligent and socially-aware poetry at various venues, often by performing pieces from his relationship-based collection, *Love is So Cool.*

Engineer by day, spoken-word artist by night, **Sutichai Savathasuk,** Mr. Chai Tea, crawls through mics in LA, sharing stories of vulnerability and humor through comedy and poetry. You can catch him playing board games, climbing rocks, and drinking milk teas in his free time.

Takayla P. Carlton, a poet and actress originally from the Midwest, draws from her diverse experiences and identities to amplify marginalized voices, particularly within women, queer, and black communities. She finds joy in her family, running, fishing, and acting, and leverages her theatre degree to explore the connection between art, identity, and self-expression in her work.

Tichina Ward-Pratt is a math teacher in South LA, mixologist, and poet searching the universe for infinite inspiration. She was born and raised in Oakland, California and is the author of the soon to be published book, *The Wounds Between Our Stars.*

Tom Meschery played basketball in the NBA from 1961–1971 with the San Francisco Warriors and Seattle Supersonics. "In the ensuing 50-plus years, I've written poems about many different subjects, but I'd bet the bank no one has written more poems about sports than me, especially about basketball."

Tommy Domino 'Alias Big Six' is a blues poet who resides in Long Beach, California. He has been teaching the Long Beach Chapter of the Community Literature Initiative since 2020. His book *Switches Hot Wheel Tracks and Extension Cords* was published by World Stage Press in 2018.

Troy R. Legette is a writer, poet, author, and actor. He's originally from Trenton, New Jersey and currently resides in Central Florida. He believes his writing will provide those in need with the therapy to uplift and heal wounds, and educate based on real-life experiences and dialogue.

Tyler Lenn Bradley (she/her) is a performance poet and mental health advocate whose debut collection, *Phasing Freely,* explores mental health through the phases of the moon. You can join Tyler on her journey by visiting www.TylerLennBradley.com.

Willie June Landers (Frank Haynes, Jr.) is a Boogie Woogie New Orleans man. He attended prestigious universities but is most comfortable in the kitchen. His greatest pleasure is experienced when people, especially females, appreciate his cuisine. Bon appetit!

When not serving the South Los Angeles community with his philanthropic work, **Woodrow Bailey** is busy documenting those who have no voice or choice in society.

Wyatt Underwood has been participating in the Los Angeles poetic communities since late January 2010. He has published six books of poems and has had a collection of his poems published by World Stage Press. He co-hosts an open mic at the Westwood, California, Branch Library.

Wynter Eddins, an author and spoken word poet, shines light on the resilience of BIPOC women through her storytelling and nonprofit, Simply Youth Institute, fostering youth empowerment and transformation.

Other Books by Mama's Kitchen Press

If you enjoyed this book, please consider checking out some of our others.
Readers like you allow us to keep our kitchen cooking
with wonderful books. Thank you!

I'm Writing to Tell You, Jaha Zainabu
Sown in Light: poetry for the forgotten soul, Tekira Briscoe
Just Be Honest: a poetic invitation to liberation, Alexander James
Sorority of Bereaved Mothers, Edited By Camari Carter Hawkins
and October B.L.U.

Available at www.mamaskitchenpress.com